The Day TWO Teams Died

Roy Cavanagh MBE & Carl Abbott

ISBN-10; 1983436143
ISBN-13: 978-1983436147

DEDICATION

This book is dedicated to all the casualties of the Munich air disaster.

In memory of the journalists that died that day, half of all proceeds from this book will go to the Journalists' Charity.
http://www.journalistscharity.org.uk/

CONTENTS

ACKNOWLEDGMENTS

Both Roy Cavanagh MBE and Carl Abbott would like to thank Tom Clarke, Leslie Millman, Trinity Mirror, The Daily Express, The Daily Mail, The Guardian and News Licensing for their help and support in this venture. We would like to pay particular thanks to David Walker, of the Daily Mirror, for his moral and practical support.

We hope that we have paid our deep respect to all involved in the Munich air disaster, particularly the brilliant journalists and reporting staff on that fateful flight.

FOREWORD

By David Walker (Sports Editor, Daily Mirror)

As a son of Manchester, born in the Fifties, it is understandable that I grew up with an awareness of events at Munich in February 1958. The fact that the disaster occurred on my birthday has ensured that throughout my life birthday celebrations have coincided with events to mark a tragedy that while largely seen as affecting Manchester United also had a much wider impact on followers of football around the world.

The loss of eight brilliant young footballers, all members of the reigning champions of England, created an emotional tsunami. Their talent, youthfulness and the fact we will never know how great they would become, undoubtedly adds to the legend surrounding Matt Busby and his thrilling young team. But the roll call of emerging stars who died on that snowbound runway, or in Duncan Edwards' case 15 days later, reflects only part of the real tragedy.

The loss of secretary Walter Crickmer, trainer Tom Curry and coach Bert Whalley can only have exacerbated the chasm United faced as they attempted to get over the tragedy of losing so many key personnel.

As the former Chairman of the Sports Journalists' Association of Great Britain I was drawn by the work the authors have done in providing an insight into the eight journalists who lost their lives on that treacherous Munich runway. This is a book of social history, revealing the life and times of the men who earned their livings reporting on sport in general and, in particular, Manchester United. The research and details Carl and Roy deliver are in equal measure fascinating and revealing.

Sixty years ago the social strata linking players, football management and the media was very different. It was the Daily Mirror's Archie Ledbrooke who lived in leafy Bramhall while Matt Busby and his players lived around Chorlton-cum-Hardy and the inner city. And one of Archie's teenage daughters was away on a skiing holiday in Switzerland when her father died in Munich. A hint of a very different lifestyle in 1958 for the girl whose father had been Chairman of the Football Writers' and Cricket Writers' associations.

Back in the Fifties the most controversial man in the press box was Henry Rose of the Daily Express. He was sartorially elegant, drove to matches in his Jaguar car and his arrival in the press box, usually with a cigar jutting from his mouth, would be announced over the club PA system. At this time the only United player with a car was skipper Roger Byrne who drove a Morris Minor 1000. Often the first sight of Henry would trigger abuse from some supporters, especially at Anfield. Henry didn't mind. He loved his notoriety and would lift his hat to salute the jeering audience.

Rose's funeral was attended by 4000 people in Manchester. Taxi drivers offered mourners free rides to the Southern Cemetery.

These were the days before 24-hour rolling sports news channels, the internet and social media. In the Fifties fans fed their hunger for sports news from their newspapers - local and national. In these post-war years the British print media never had it so good.

Today one of the issues the SJA has fought for is to prevent the exploitation of young journalists who are desperate to get a chance in the game. Many are lured into working for little or no return for the experience of seeing their work published or online. I hope they will read this book and recognise the role their forefathers played in a golden era for the written media.

Some of the writing can be criticised now - such as referring to a Dublin-born player as British - but there are also exquisite insights into that era.

In part this book honours the memory of the men who created a piece of perfect sporting shorthand, a title that eloquently described the individual parts of a team made whole. The eight journalists who died at Munich were among those who created the name that lives on sixty years later - The Busby Babes.

Half of the profits from this book will go to the Journalists' Charity. It was launched in 1864 when a group of parliamentary journalists, including Charles Dickens, set up a fund to help their colleagues and dependents who had fallen on hard times. Since then, the charity has assisted those most in need with financial help as well as residential and nursing care.

December, 2017.

INTRODUCTION

When the Elizabethan 'Lord Burleigh' G-ALZU AS57 aircraft, British Airways flight 609, attempted its fateful third take off at Munich airport on the afternoon of Thursday 6th February 1958, it did not just seal the fate of seven Manchester United footballers: Roger Byrne; Eddie Colman; Mark Jones; Liam (Billy) Whelan; Tommy Taylor; David Pegg and Geoff Bent, then the cream of one of England's greatest ever football sides, known via the name of their manager as the 'Busby Babes'. Some of Britain's finest sporting journalists were also cruelly lost to the world. Eight of them perished: Alf Clarke (Manchester Evening Chronicle); Don Davies (Manchester Guardian); Tom Jackson (Manchester Evening News); George Follows (Daily Herald); Archie Ledbrooke (Daily Mirror); Henry Rose (Daily Express); Eric Thompson (Daily Mail) and Frank Swift (News of the World).

An eighth Manchester United footballer, regarded as one of England's greatest ever players and then still only 21 years of age, Duncan Edwards, died fifteen days later from his terrible injuries. The manager of this star studded side, Matt Busby, was fighting for his life, whilst two of his trusted backroom staff, Bert Whalley and Tom Curry and the man who made the club tick over, Walter Crickmer, the club secretary, had also been killed outright on February 6. The co-pilot Captain Ken Rayment and steward W.T. (Tommy) Cable, along with Willie Satinoff, expected to be a future Manchester United director, and Mr Bela Miklos, the club's travel agent, made the total twenty two fatalities on the day, which increased to twenty three on Duncan Edwards' passing.

There had actually been nine journalists on the charter flight, returning from covering the European Cup quarter final. The second leg tie had been played in Belgrade the previous day, and had seen Manchester United qualify for the semi-finals with a 3-3 draw and a 5-4 aggregate victory against Yugoslav champions Red Star Belgrade. As noted, eight journalists were killed, the ninth, Frank Taylor of the News Chronicle-Dispatch, was lying in the Rechts der Isar Hospital in Munich fighting for his life with critical injuries. He thankfully survived and continued to be a fine, respected journalist.

Back in 1958 people were reliant on newspaper journalists to tell them what was really happening in the world. Those journalists killed and badly injured at Munich were literally the voice of sport for the masses. Their offices reflected the importance of journalism, for the time they were sumptuous providing the men who wrote the words the people wanted, and needed to know. Social Media would not be created for another fifty years! Television had only really become available to most people after the Coronation of Princess Elizabeth II had been televised in 1953. Radio, though, was very popular and a real source of news and entertainment. The newspapers though, and there was quite a few of them, two evening papers alone in Manchester at the time, the Evening News and Evening Chronicle, were eagerly read to update on local and world news, and the happenings of the local sporting teams in particular. Eight of those newspapers had their top sports journalists wiped out at the end of the Munich airport runway on Thursday 6th February 1958.

As mentioned, one man Frank Taylor, survived. He actually would return to journalism and, indeed, wrote the definitive account of the tragedy in a book called 'The Day a Team Died'. The happenings at Munich actually seemed to transform Manchester United, already a well-known football club, into one of the world's most famous football clubs. The stories about the players who died have been well documented, This, though, is a tribute to the brilliant writers who wrote about a brilliant team.

CHAPTER ONE
A GREAT DISASTER FOR JOURNALISM

IN MEMORIAM

ALFRED CLARKE
(Manchester Evening Chronicle)

HARRY DONALD DAVIES
(Manchester Guardian)

GEORGE ALBERT FOLLOWS
(Daily Herald)

THOMAS WILLIAM JACKSON
(Manchester Evening News)

ARCHIBALD WILLIAM LEDBROOKE
(Daily Mirror)

HENRY ROSE
(Daily Express)

FRANK VICTOR SWIFT
(News of the World)

ERIC THOMPSON
(Daily Mail)

ST. BRIDE'S CHURCH, FLEET STREET

Tuesday, 25th February, 1958 at 12.30 p.m.

Conducted by the Rector
THE REV. CYRIL M. ARMITAGE,
M.V.O., M.A.
and
THE REV. CANON C. B. MORTLOCK,
M.A., F.S.A.

Figure 1 Fleet Street Memorial

Let us now look in detail at the eight journalists who lost their lives at the end of Munich airport's runway on Thursday 6th February 1958. A chapter on each of them, putting in some of their prose on how Manchester United's young players had developed and bloomed, starting alphabetically with Alf Clarke.

ALF CLARKE
'HE BLED MANCHESTER UNITED RED BLOOD'

ALF CLARKE WAS UNITED

Figure 2 Manchester Evening Chronicle, February 7, 1958

Figure 3 Alf Clarke

"The man bled Manchester United red blood". That statement emphasises the total dedication that Alf Clarke had about Manchester United. Such was that dedication that Alf was a shareholder in United and Vice-President of the Manchester United Supporters' Club. He was the main reporter of the club for the Manchester Evening Chronicle, where he would publish the latest news nightly Monday to Saturday, then follow up in their Saturday night sports version called the 'Football Pink'. He also had a page in the club's football programme, the 'United Review' which was first issued in August 1932 as a chronicle of the club's activities, events and all the match day information needed. Though It was called 'Casual Comments', it was much more than that as Alf astutely managed to intertwine the present day with happenings of the past. Very friendly with club secretary, Walter Crickmer, Alf was privy to all dealings really with Manchester United, on and off the pitch. A very smartly dressed man, who along with Matt Busby was the greatest public advocate Manchester United could ever have had.

He was, therefore, in a privileged position to witness at first hand the club's promotion of young players following on from the very successful, but aging, post war side of Johnny Carey, Stan Pearson, Jack Rowley etc. Here are his views on that side and some of the young, developing players such as Dennis Viollet and Duncan Edwards.

As early as 1946 Alf Clarke spotted the potential of Dennis Viollet in the Manchester Boys versus Glasgow Boys match where he noted Dennis Viollet as a 'Boy with a Future', prophetically claiming that he was a future international, which he actually would be but amazingly only twice in his marvellous career. 'This was Viollet's match' he wrote. 'In the full bloom of youthful soccer craftsmanship, Viollet promises to bloom into one of the games stars' Dennis scored two in Manchester Boys resounding 6-2 victory over their Scottish counterparts.

Towards the end of the 1952/3 season, Alf Clarke had been to watch a Manchester United side play Ashton United in the final of the Gilgryst Cup. The match, played at the club's famous training ground in Salford called The Cliff, witnessed a quite brilliant display from a young lad of 16 years 185 days

6

old called Duncan Edwards. Only three days later Alf was present at Old Trafford to see the same Duncan Edwards make his full United debut in a match against Cardiff City. In the later edition of the paper that evening which then became 'The Pink', Alf Clarke wrote; *'The only ray of sunshine that filtered through the United gloom as they slumped to a 1-4 defeat, was the display of boy debutante Duncan Edwards, who did all that could be asked of him, including taking a shot from 30 yards that was only just wide.'* These words of praise were alongside an action picture of young Duncan on the front page, while more encouraging words were written in the match report on the centre pages. In his report, Clarke continued, *'Edwards had the right ideas when he tried another long range effort and was instrumental in setting United on the move with a glorious pass up the middle arising from which Berry forced a corner.'*

Alf Clarke witnessed the blooming of the young talent he had been reporting on with great pride as they began to make their mark in the first team. The actual remark 'Busby Babes' is sometimes attributed to both Alf and Tom Jackson, but certainly the Manchester Evening Chronicle's sports paper (Football Pink) for Saturday 31st October 1953 had the headline *'Busby's Bouncing Babes Keep All Town Awake'.* Alf Clarke could not have realised his article about a 0-0 draw away at third placed Huddersfield Town would bring the phrase 'Busby's Babes' to the attention of all football followers.

After establishing themselves in United's first team, many of the Babes established themselves as England internationals. Manchester United's trip to London in late March 1954 to play the previous season champions, Arsenal, was always part of a grand event when Manchester United were in the capital. Even more so at that grandest of all football stadiums, Highbury. The charisma of the two clubs just made it a hot ticket to have for all football fans and all celebrities it seemed. The game fell on the same day as the two FA Cup semi-finals played that day and the fact that the then England team manager, Walter Winterbottom, a former United player himself, had decided to go to Highbury instead of either semi-final was a hint, certainly as far as Alf Clarke was concerned, that the form of Duncan Edwards was on the England manager's mind with the forthcoming Scotland versus England match due. In his Manchester Evening Chronicle article of the day he reflected, *'Edwards, as big as a tank and as tough as Wilf Copping, is the greatest of England's post war finds. In West Germany for an under 23 International recently, he put in tackles that put the continentals completely off their game; and when he cleared the ball he hit it really accurately to his colleagues. Given a good game today at Arsenal, he starts favourite for the left half position in the full England side'.*

As it was, United lost to Arsenal and young Duncan would have to wait another year for his England debut but, obviously, Roger Byrne impressed the England manager as he was selected for his international debut against Scotland.

Early in 1955, Alf Clarke laid it on the line how far he felt Duncan Edwards would go in the game, in Alf's opinion he was a future England captain as his article in the 'Football Pink' during March 1955 stated, *'The chief problem about Duncan is where do you play him? He is already a brilliant wing half who can also play centre half, now both United and England via the U23's have placed him in their attack. We cannot escape the fact that Duncan Edwards is the greatest young player of his age. He is a future England captain.'*

MANCHESTER UNITED SUPPORTERS' CLUB

Headquarters: G.P.O. SOCIAL CLUB, BROWN STREET, MANCHESTER, 2
Affiliated to the National Federation of Football Supporters' Clubs

TO HELP   NOT HINDER

Vice-Presidents:
ALF. CLARKE (Deceased), COUNCILLOR EDWARD REID (Stretford), W. LINGLEY, Esq., H. HORROCKS, Esq.

Chairman:	Secretary:	Treasurer:
HAROLD POWELL	DEREK N. BURBIDGE	JOE OGDEN

Vice-Chairman:	Social Secretary:
MAJOR HARRY RAWCLIFFE	HARRY THORP

Management Committee
Consists of all the above together with Representatives from the following Branches: Ashton, Openshaw, Stretford, Salford, Crumpsall, Eccles and District, Peel Green, Cheetham Hill, Collyhurst, Central, Droylsden, Moston.

Editor: D. N. BURBIDGE

Figure 4 Excerpt from Manchester United Supporters' Club Memorial Handbook showing Alf Clark as Vice-President

Alf Clarke had joined the Evening Chronicle as a boy on leaving Manchester Grammar School at the age of sixteen. He had served in the war in the Flying Corps as a pilot officer. Married, the couple had a married daughter and a son who was serving in the Army at the time of Alf's death. His ashes were scattered on the Old Trafford pitch towards the Stretford End, a fitting resting place for a man who lived Manchester United.

H.D. (Donny) DAVIES
'OLD INTERNATIONAL'

Figure 5 - Manchester Guardian, February 7, 1958

"OLD INTERNATIONAL"
H. D. Davies : a man who loved sport

Figure 6 HD 'Donny' Davies

Don Davies was a small, smiling, cloth capped man of Victorian virtues, having a broad range of accomplishments and being of rich literary talent. He was actually a man of many talents, he played amateur international football for England and League football for Bolton Wanderers and appeared at cricket for the Lancashire County side, also appearing with distinction in the local cricket leagues, particularly with Bradshaw Cricket Club in the Bolton League. He was an acclaimed broadcaster with people eagerly looking forward to hearing his comments every Saturday. He was such a revered journalist, writing under the name of 'Old International' he was often spoken of in the same breath as his Manchester Guardian contemporary Neville Cardus. Indeed, Cardus wrote about his colleague, *'He was the first writer on soccer to rise above the immediate and quickly perishable levels of his theme and give us something to preserve. Old International was not only the best of soccer reporters, he was something of a poet.'*

Donny was born in Pendleton, Salford in 1892. His father, brought up in an orphanage, showed massive determination to make a fine life for himself, ending up as a mill manager in Bolton. Don Davies had a fine education at Bolton School, playing football first for Northern Nomads, then going on an England amateur international tour of Austria, Hungary and Romania, also later playing against Wales. When war broke out in 1914, he signed up with the Officer Training Corps, serving as an infantry lieutenant, finally going in the Royal Flying Corps. His service started disastrously as having just gained his wings, Donny Davies was shot down and captured by the Germans. Spending time in prison camps he suffered so badly that he lost so much weight he was only given six months to live on his repatriation.

The drive and determination that Donny Davies would show throughout his entire life was never seen better than when he decided that he had to get a job, so studying for a University degree at night was accompanied by starting work in the Education Department with the Manchester Engineering firm Mather & Platt. He would stay there until his retirement in 1957. That, along with his lifetime vocation of helping young people learn would have been enough for most, not for Donny Davies though!

Marriage to Gertrude in 1921 brought them two daughters. This, along with his love of music, dance, art and poetry, during which he saw all the famous practitioners of the day from Barbiroli to Nijinsky, his involvement with the scouting movement, his playing football and cricket at a high level, and of course his work with Mather & Platt brought him a very full life. By 1932, all these interests had to take second place to his writing as his first piece appeared in the Manchester Guardian.

Don Davies besides his sporting prowess was a very accomplished after-dinner speaker, and a fine broadcaster who replaced an equally fine broadcaster called Tom Clegg. They both had a natural talent that endeared them to their many listeners.

His view of Duncan Edwards in one of his early display for Manchester United in November 1953 quickly spotted the immense talent Duncan had. United's very young side played Blackpool, the holders of the FA Cup following their thrilling 4-3 victory the previous May against Bolton Wanderers at Wembley Stadium. Don, under his 'Old International' banner for the Manchester Guardian found plenty of space to praise both Duncan and his young team mates. He likened the display of the half back line to that of the vintage Duckworth, Roberts and Bell trio of the early 1900's. Duncan Edwards was particularly praised for the way he played against that excellent inside right Ernie Taylor, *'that to get into the picture at all, Ernie Taylor had to wander far away from his youthful opponent. This 17 year old left half gives the lie direct to the adage that old heads do not grow on young shoulders. There seems little that time and experience can add to his present store of shrewdness and judgement, unless it be the reminder that there is such a thing as beginner's luck.'*

Duncan Edwards, of course, was not going to need beginners luck as he quickly developed into a quite magnificent left half. Donny Davies though, was a marvellous journalist and he could add comments which player's did well to take heed of when it was required. Duncan Edwards was no exception! Following his first Manchester 'Derby' against City at Old Trafford Donny Davies reflected that, *'where was Edwards when McAdams moved in to collect Clarke's cross, why was he alone? Another curious thing. Though Edwards was seeing as much of the ball as any player, his outside left Pegg spent far too much time kicking his toes in idleness. Yet his service to Taylor and across field to Berry were beyond praise. But why neglect his own wing so much?'* Such criticism in no way reduced the admiration Don Davies had for Duncan Edwards though. An admiration which continued throughout the player's career. A typical quote which epitomised Duncan and also the marvellous writing of Donny Davies was this in a match against Arsenal, *'Edwards had time to hurl himself at the rebound and fill the Arsenal goalmouth with the dust from a monstrous and explosive shot.'*

Don Davies did not put one word in an article when he could put two, and the extra words always added to a very descriptive article. He was an essayist more than he was a reporter. Take for example, another quote on Duncan Edwards by Donny describing how Duncan got his first goal for Manchester United against Blackpool on January 1st 1955, Donny Davies reported, *'By common consent, the outstanding incident of a somewhat desultory second half was the scoring of Edwards' first goal for United. Ever since he had pulled on a red jersey over his muscular frame, this lusty 17 year old has dreamt of one thing only; namely to smite a ball so hard that it wither bursts in transit or defies the efforts of any goalkeeper to intercept it. On Saturday, with about twenty minutes left, Edwards at last detected his opportunity. Darting forward, he put every ounce of his prodigious strength into the mighty uninhibited swipe. There was a sharp crack of the boot on leather-veritable detonation this-and a clearing of the atmosphere by a blurred effect, which first soared over Farm's upraised arms in the Blackpool goal then dipped suddenly and passed under the crossbar. Edwards leaped and gambolled like a soul possessed until his adoring colleagues fell upon him and pinned him down with their embraces.'*

There are a few stories of how journalists who actually travelled to Belgrade, might not have gone. One such was at the Guardian where John

Figure 7 Donny Davies with Alf Clarke & Frank Taylor (behind) returning from Madrid

Arlott wanted to extend his coverage of football and actually covered the Arsenal v Manchester United match at Highbury on February 1, 1958. He was told he was going to cover the Red Star v Manchester United European Cup tie the following Wednesday until on the Sunday, Donny Davies requested that he cover the match with his local Manchester side. The following Thursday, a disconsolate John Arlott was mooching around a London bookshop when his office tracked him down to inform of the crash and he had to prepare an obituary for Donny Davies.

GEORGE FOLLOWS
'THE WORKING MAN'S JOURNALIST'

Figure 8 - George Follows

● The Old Trafford motto:
CONCILIO ET LABORE . . .
" Planning and effort."

Follows
was with
HIS team

*Figure 9 Daily Herald
February 7, 1958*

'A very fine wordsmith' is a fitting tribute to George, a man from the Walsall area, who displayed all those qualities in his much read writing. Some of his friends felt he was so good on anything he turned his hand to that he didn't seem to have to try hard to succeed. He would mature into a very fine writer.

It was after leaving Queen Mary Grammar School in Walsall that George started working for the local Walsall Times, before moving to the Wolverhampton Express & Star a few years before the start of the Second World War. His writing came to a much larger public when he joined the Daily Herald's Manchester offices, and began his reporting of the local North West football scene. He would have started writing about the Third Division (North),with his choice of spectacles going from the steel rimmed services type glasses of the time to majestically horn rimmed glasses as he then arrived writing about the best players, the best matches.

Roy Cavanagh recalls *'as a youngster growing up in what would now be classed as a Salford slum, but not to those of us living in them at the time, they were just our houses, the only papers I saw were the two, then, Manchester Evening papers, the News and the Chronicle, along with the working man's news, the Daily Herald. Being young, it was to the sports pages I gravitated, and the Herald's main sports reporter was George Follows'.*

England had a great victory over West Germany in Berlin in May 1956. West Germany were then the World Cup holders and an England team, containing three Manchester United players, Roger Byrne, Tommy Taylor and Duncan Edwards went over there and beat them comfortably 3-1. George Follows covered the match and reported on Taylor and Edwards thus. *'The Germans thought Taylor was WUNDERBAR! His movement was majestic, his courage tremendous. Yet he is not perfectly fit. He has had a thigh muscle trouble since last August. On coach rides he sits on his hands to ease the pain. He will become the greatest centre forward in the world.'*

On Duncan Edwards, who scored a memorable goal, George Follows reported, *'Edwards went through like a tank in the 25th minute, destroyed four tackles and bombed in a goal he had threatened all this summer tour for England. Ninety Thousand Germans shuddered every time Duncan got the ball.'*

In 1957, George Follows actually helped out the Manchester United players as they turned their hand to journalism. The team had reached the 1957 FA Cup Final against Aston Villa, at one stage it could have been part of a treble of League, FA Cup and European Cup, 42 years before another

breed of Manchester United stars actually achieved the feat. As footballers were still on the minimum wage then, any extra cash was warmly accepted. A leading Manchester bookmaker, Johnny Foy, offered to get some of his business contacts to advertise whilst Dennis Viollet and Ray Wood turned their hands to writing instead of scoring and saving goals respectively, to create the 40-page brochure. This was where George Follows came in as he offered to put it all together and his Daily Herald newspaper helped by advertising it in their paper, through shops and through their newspaper lads. It cost 2s 6d (12.5p) to buy.

Figure 10 Red Devils Brochure (1957)

The title of the brochure *The Red Devils* leads to another of George's claims to fame. George is credited in the Manchester United Supporters Club Memorial Brochure in 1958 with having introduced the phrase. In their tribute to George they say *'George Fellows was modest when he had so much reason to be proud of his talents. Yet there was one term he introduced that he was proud to hold as his copyright – "The Red Devils".'* It is a phrase he repeats throughout his reports at a time when they were generally referred to by others as the Babes.

Of all the interesting articles one report by George Follows of a conversation with Matt Busby in Brussels where they had seen Athletic Bilbao beat Hungarian Champions Honved, who had to play away from the Budapest home, to qualify to play United in the European Cup quarter finals stands out.

'I asked Matt whether he would be interested in signing the famous Hungarian player Puskas as the Honved team were deciding to try and play elsewhere in Europe as opposed to go back to their troubled country. Matt replied, "I will not be signing Puskas". It was further confirmation that Matt Busby was more than happy with his wonderful young devils.'

After the Cup Final, Dennis and Ray went to the Daily Herald offices just off Oxford Road to collect their money. The money was all in coins; threepenny bits, sixpences, shillings and half-crowns and had all been stored in one of those big newspaper bags that the sellers used to wield around town at the time. Ray Wood recalled; *'It was blooming heavy I can tell you, we couldn't lift it.'* The two Manchester United stars certainly startled onlookers as they watched in amazement as the two well-known players dragged the bag down the steps onto the pavement and into a taxi. Ray continued,

'Johnny Foy had organised for his bank to let us go in by the side entrance where they counted the money for us, although it could have looked as though two blokes were actually returning a bank raid to a bank! Sadly, we only sold 6,000 copies of the brochure with us having to get rid of about 30,000 copies as we had wildly over estimated.'

Mind you, they would have been worth a bit today on the memorabilia market! Ray Wood, of course, suffered a really bad injury in that 1957 Final when, with no substitutes allowed in those days, Aston Villa beat a virtual ten man Manchester United 2-1, whilst the quite brilliant Dennis Viollet could not shake off an injury, giving a young Bobby Charlton his final place.

Matt Busby and George Follows fly to another European Cup adventure. Here, George Follows, Daily Herald football reporter, recaptures some of the thrills of United's epic season.

Figure 11 George Follows with Sir Matt Busby from his Red Devils brochure

George Follows was considered the finest sporting journalist by many, brilliant, witty, satirical and always honest. A big friend of Jimmy Murphy, imagine what it must have been like to sit and listen to their conversations together. Red Devil George had two dreams for his beloved *'Red Devils'*. One for Manchester United to win the European Cup, the other for his then ten year old son Richard, to become one of those Red Devils.

TOM JACKSON
'UNITED JOTTINGS'

Figure 12 Manchester Evening News, February 7,

Man who lived for United

Figure 13
Tom Jackson

Like his colleague Alf Clarke, Tom Jackson wrote in one of the two Manchester evening newspapers, in Tom's case the Evening News, and also in the famous club programme, "The United Review" where he wrote a 'United Topics' column, both combining the role of updating the Manchester public of the daily happenings at Manchester United. He was a smaller man height-wise than Clarke, but a burly figure who had covered Manchester United since 1934, when Tom had been twenty two years of age. Tom actually joined the Evening News when he was fourteen quickly wanting to become a reporter. He had to break off from that role during the Second World War as he moved into intelligence work tracking Nazi war criminals during the war. In one instance, Tom was one of a small squad in Germany who unmasked Irma Grese the notorious woman Nazi torturer of Belsen. She was working alongside Tom Jackson posing as a 'freed German' but she was detected, put on trial and executed.

As with Alf Clarke, Tom's role changed from part time work reporting Manchester United alongside news stories, to a full-time role as the fortunes of the football club soared. No two people scrutinised the transition from the post war team towards a team built on Matt's principle of youth and the emergence of the Busby Babes more closely than Alf Clarke and Tom Jackson of the Manchester Chronicle and Evening News respectively. Between them, they take credit for the immortal phase 'The Busby Babes'.

How much would a modern day advertising company pay for the phrase 'The Busby Babes'? Well the first known use of the word 'Babes' in conjunction with United was the heading of a match report from November 24, 1951 by Tom Jackson when United played away at Anfield against Liverpool. The game saw the debuts of Roger Byrne (21) and Jackie Blanchflower (18) and is widely acknowledged as the genesis of the Babes, it read, 'United's "Babes" Cool, Confident'. A couple of famous names in the Liverpool side were Bob Paisley, their future manager, and Billy Liddell one of Liverpool's all-time greats.

Being so close to the daily activities at Old Trafford, Tom Jackson was privy to the latest news. Even he though could not have realised that the news he broke on 4th April 1953 would herald the start of, arguably, the truly great career of a Manchester United footballer, the debut of Duncan Edwards. Tom was able to record the personal touch of Duncan reporting that morning with the other ground staff 16 year olds, only to be told by Matt Busby he would be making his first team debut against Cardiff City. Obviously thrilled, Duncan evidentially asked for permission to ring his parents about his debut before he went home to his digs and told his landlady Mrs Watson, who also had the likes of Jackie Blanchflower, David Pegg and Mark Jones living there.

Ever the perfectionist, Tom Jackson had encountered real problems in Bilbao in January 1957 as Manchester United played a vital European Cup match against the local Athletic team. He had been in touch with the local British Consul and local technicians to make sure there would not be a hitch. As Bilbao swept into an early lead Tom was stood at one end of the press box jabbering away to Manchester, when he kept hearing another voice down the line, an English voice! As he shouted down the line for him to shut up he turned round to see, stood at the other end of the room his colleague Alf Clarke of the other Manchester Evening paper of the time. Tom walked down the room tapping Alf on the shoulder, only to be told to go away as he was sending his story back to Manchester and that Tom should know better. It was then that Tom informed Alf that he was actually sending his match report down the line to him! Luckily, and quickly, both men got lines to send information as the match went from 3-0 to the home side to 3-2 then back out to 5-2 before Billy Whelan scored a magnificent late goal to give United a sporting chance in the second leg.

During September 1957, Duncan Edwards celebrated his twenty first birthday, and Tom Jackson noted the landmark for the young man by saying in the club programme *'it is just four and half years since Duncan Edwards made his league debut for Manchester United, but what a crowded and memorable soccer life he has packed in between. Not many professionals of Duncan's age will ever experience such a rapid rise to the top'*

Manchester United had tried a few penalty takers over the Busby Babes period, Roger Byrne, Johnny Berry both had times as the regular taker. After a vital miss away at West Bromwich Albion in November 1957 by Berry, Matt Busby decided that a change was needed with Duncan Edwards being given the job. He was not going to mess about was Duncan as he showed against Bolton Wanderers at Old Trafford in mid-January 1958, and how he took that penalty! Tom Jackson recalled, *'Since taking over from Johnny Berry, Duncan gives a penalty a real bash as England goalkeeper Eddie Hopkinson found out. He had already let six in so to see big Duncan stepping forward to take a penalty which would make it seven, it was lucky it did not take his head off as it fairly whistled into the net, threatening to take the same netting with it'*

Tom Jackson's only son, Mike, was only eleven at the time of the crash, attending Mauldeth Road Primary in Fallowfield, and was coming home from school when the news of the crash started to hit the news boards. Getting home to a then already crowded house of family, and friends, it was later that night that the devastating news was confirmed of Tom's death.

As a lasting tribute by the Manchester Evening News to honour their lead sports reporter, they commissioned a brass engraved plaque, which was originally hung on the wall near to where Tom sat penning his many Manchester United reports. It was transferred to the new offices in Deansgate, then to No1 Scott Place in Spinningfields, finally to Chadderton. It was fitting that his son, Mike, was able to show his son and daughter the memorial to a marvellous journalist.

Back Row : Tommy Jackson, Frank Taylor, George Follows, David Jack.
Seated : Eric THOMPSON, Henry Rose, Alf Clarke, Frank McGhee.
Front : Bill Gregory.

Figure 14 Tom Jackson with colleagues, Dublin September 1957

Tom Jackson was a man who had reported on Manchester United from their Second Division days, then even hanging by a thread to avoid going down to the Third Division, before the return started before the Second World War, right through to the creation of the team known as the 'Busby Babes'. He is a fitting example to any young person wanting to follow journalism, and it was fitting that the Sports Editor finished his obituary note by calling Tom, "The Master Reporter."

ARCHIE LEDBROOKE
'THE MAN IN THE MIRROR'

Figure 16 Archie Ledbrooke

Figure 15 Daily Mirror, February 7, 1958

THE MAN WHO LIVED AND DIED FOR SPORT

A tall, very authoritative man in all that he did, he was married to Eileen, and they would have two daughters, Jane born in 1934 and Helen in 1938. During the Second World War, Archie would reach the rank of Captain during his time with the Intelligence Corps.

He had started his journalistic career in local Surrey papers before he moved to Bristol then onto the busy Manchester journalistic hub. The Daily Dispatch was followed by one of the two evening papers in the city then, the Evening News was where Archie landed where he became an accomplished sports writer. When he moved to the Daily Mirror in November 1955 he would become their chief sports reporter, earning the by line 'He is the sports writer you MUST NOT MISS', emphasising the power and attraction of journalists, who were almost as popular as the sporting stars they were writing about. A few years earlier for instance Archie Ledbrooke and Edgar Turner had written an excellent football book called 'Soccer from the Press Box' which had really covered all aspects of journalism and the stories behind the famous names in the game going back to the turn of the century. Other books by Archie included 'Lancashire County Cricket Club', 'Great Moments in Sport' and 'The Fight for The Ashes 1948'

People sometimes mistakenly thought he was aloof, but Archie, known to his friends as 'Laddy', fitted in with ease really amongst the Manchester press corps. Once a game was over he loved nothing more than rushing back to Bramhall to have a bite to eat then off with Eileen to play a game of bridge.

Besides football, he was a very fine reporter of cricket, which was probably his first love. He would have many a discussion with Donny Davies analysing the merits of the players on the county and Test scene. This love of both sports was reflected by the enormous honour of being Chairman of both the Football Writers Association and the Cricket Writers Club - the only man to have been voted into these two offices.

Whilst Archie was detailed to cover the Red Star Belgrade v Manchester United match in Belgrade, he had also promised his sports editor, Peter Wilson, that he would finish his article on the Blackpool manager Joe Smith who had led Blackpool to their only FA Cup Final triumph when they beat Bolton Wanderers 4-3 in an amazing 1953 final, dubbed the Stanley

Matthews final, although Stan Mortensen had become the only man to score an hat trick in a final in the same game. Joe Smith himself had known how to win cup finals as he had appeared in two for Bolton Wanderers in the mid 1920's. Archie Ledbrooke really wanted to do this article as he had a great deal of time for Joe Smith, although the Daily Mirror had Frank McGhee on standby to travel to Belgrade if Archie did not manage his deadline. In the event he sent the article over and McGhee actually covered the World Cup qualifying game between Wales and Israel, a game in which the United assistant manager Jimmy Murphy was managing the Wales side as they looked to reach the finals for the first time.

On the day of the crash, Archie Ledbrooke's daughters were in different countries. Jane was skiing in Switzerland whilst Helen was out shopping locally with her mother. When they arrived back at their Bramhall home, near Stockport, they were soon being called by a neighbour who asked had they heard the news about the Manchester United plane crash? They had obviously not heard at that time and just could not take the shocking news in. Jane was equally devastated being over in Switzerland and immediately made arrangements to return home.

A couple of days after the crash, Helen was to receive a postcard from Belgrade showing the River Danube on the front and the following message from her father on the back. "This is the famous Blue Danube River not much snow here but plenty on the way" signed, "Love Daddy".

Archie Ledbrooke was buried in Bramhall, and as with all the other fatalities, the funerals drew major crowds of people wanting to pay their respect. The family got the medical report from the crash which informed them that Archie had been killed instantly. The family's only solace being that he would have hated being an invalid, often recalling that Archie saying he didn't mind death, but he hated being ill. The reminders though became too much to bear at times for the close-knit family, so a relocation as far away from the Manchester area as they could, led to a new beginning 250 miles away in Chichester, Sussex.

HENRY ROSE
'Mr CHARISMA'

SPORTS KING OF THE NORTH

Figure 17
Daily Express, February 7, 1958

Figure 18 Henry Rose

The first thing to say about Henry Rose is that he was such a showman that his controversies, whilst annoying many who read his views, they could not help but buy the paper the following day to see what he was saying now!. His fame was such that he was as famous as the footballing stars he reported on.

Born in Norwich in 1899 to his Ukrainian-Jewish migrant father and mother, Woolf and Esther Rose. It was not long into the twentieth century though that the family moved to live in Cardiff. Henry was enlisted to serve in the First World War, commenting, *'lived and died a hundred times during those agonising times. The wind howled, shells whistled over my head, my brain was just numb. I could not help feel helplessness, slowly becoming reconciled to the worst.'*

After the war Henry felt a dual ethnicity, his Jewishness embraced, rather than hid, his tireless charity and philanthropy work. Although born in Norwich he was also an extremely proud Welshman. It was in Cardiff that his journalistic career started, working for the South Wales Echo before and after World War One. In his early twenties, Henry moved across to the Western Evening Herald in Plymouth, which he called his 'journalistic nursery'. By 1926, the year of the General Strike, Henry arrived at the hotbed of journalism, the Northern Headquarters of the Daily Express. Henry Rose would stride its corridors for the next thirty two years.

Between the two wars, newspapers had a real boom, with coverage of sport seen as key in the circulation wars of that time. Henry Rose, literally, rose to the challenge with his fearsome views of major incidents, such as giving inside views on the controversial England football match in West Germany in 1938 when the team were forced by the FA, according to Henry Rose, to give the Nazi salute against their wishes. Earlier that year following the England v Scotland international at Wembley Stadium, Henry Rose reported, *'Five minutes after I had left the Wembley Stadium I had completely forgotten about the match. The worst international I had seen for years, almost ever, for long stretches my notebook lay undisturbed, as were the two goalkeepers'*

Betting on the football pools was a major source of enjoyment for the public, with such as Henry Rose giving tips and score predictions, having the public relying on giving them an inside knowledge and then, hopefully, financial interest. He also had the inside knowledge to give scoops about major transfers such as Tommy Lawton's move from Everton to Chelsea in

1945. He simply oozed personality and charisma, as he brought much needed colour into a grey world.

Figure 19 Personalised Christmas Card

As football was such a massive crowd pull after the war, there were even placards outside grounds informing 'Henry Rose is here today' with such as Liverpool's famous Spion Kop ritually booing him as he entered the Anfield press box, with Rose, arriving at the ground in his Jaguar, immaculate with a big cigar, overcoat and brown trilby hat, raising that hat to them! The public loved Henry Rose. They hated Henry Rose. But they never ignored him- Henry never gave them a chance. Remember, the giants of the sports writing press were towering figures, describing events few had seen and setting the sporting agenda with the ferocity of their views. None did it better than Henry Rose.

Munich survivor, Dennis Viollet recalled a typical story about the journalists that died and the extrovert that was Henry Rose:

"These reporters were the cream of writers. They wrote vivid descriptions about the matches they watched so that the readers felt as if they had actually been at the game themselves. There was none of the muck raking that came later in the 1960's, although if one pushed the mark with his comments it was dear old Henry Rose! He loved mixing it in his articles. I recall him being very unkind and unfair to Tommy Taylor on a few occasions. At one time Tommy had scored five goals in two England internationals, a hat-trick against the Republic of Ireland at Wembley and then a week later, two goals in Copenhagen against Denmark, both matches World Cup qualifiers, but Henry had a right go at him, saying, 'If Tommy Taylor the Manchester United centre forward was worthy of an England place, then I am Father Christmas.' All the lads were extremely annoyed with Henry and I remember Matt Busby and Jimmy Murphy having words with him. For all that though, Henry Rose liked a bit of fun. Players might not have always agreed with what he wrote but on the whole all got on with each other. They had their job to do and so had we, we respected each other'

When Wales were drawn in 1957 to play Israel in a World Cup qualifying double header, Henry Rose commenting on his dual thoughts said, 'I would be left supporting the referee!' It was ironic that on the day Henry Rose reported on his last match in Belgrade, Wales and Israel were playing their second leg tie in Cardiff, with Manchester United's assistant manager, Jimmy Murphy, leading the Wales side to victory and qualification for the forthcoming 1958 World Cup Finals in Sweden.

Figure 20 Henry Rose Press Pass (Bilbao)

Eric Cooper, of the Daily Express recalled his friend. *'It is doubtful there has been a more energetic character in newspaper journalism then Henry, who was probably better known than any writer in the sporting field. A supreme showman, with flair and flamboyance, he was a gambler, not just on cards and horses, but on people, too. They may have called him provocative, even an egotist, but he always spoke what he felt was the truth'.*

The biggest funeral of all was for Henry Rose, the most read sporting journalist. Manchester's thousand strong taxi fleet volunteered transport free for anyone who wanted to be at the Southern Cemetery funeral. It was estimated 4,000 went to it. As it was a Jewish funeral, everyone had to wear hats, people had never seen such a collection of bowlers, homburgs, caps, trilbies, headscarves, anything so people could join the six mile queue. The hearse stopped outside the Daily Express offices in Manchester and by the time it was passing close to the Maine Road stadium of Manchester City, the leading cars were already treble parked at the cemetery.

FRANK SWIFT
'A GIANT ON, AND OFF THE PITCH'

FRANK SWIFT: The Man We'll Miss But Not Forget

Figure 21 News of the World, February 9, 1958 **By THE SPORTS EDITOI**

Born in Blackpool at the outbreak of the First World War in 1914, Frank began playing goalkeeper for local clubs around Fleetwood before being spotted by Manchester City in the early 1930's. After time in their reserves Frank was given his league debut on Christmas Day 1933, he would not then be out of the City side for over four years.

Figure 22 Frank Swift

During this period Manchester City were one of the top English sides, winning the FA Cup in 1934 when they defeated Portsmouth 2-1, although a still young Frank Swift was so overcome by emotion he actually fainted at the final whistle. Whilst he recovered enough to receive his winner's medal from King George V, the King sent a telegram on the following Monday enquiring about his condition. A couple of seasons later, 1936/37, Manchester City had a poor start to the season but pulled it all around over the Christmas period. They then went on a long unbeaten run, eventually winning their first ever League Championship.

Incredibly, the following season despite scoring more goals than any other side, Manchester City were relegated. Matt Busby had played in the 1934 final, the pair becoming great friends which lasted all Frank's life. During the Second World War after joining the British Army, Frank and Matt met up many times, playing for the Army and also guesting for various teams when on leave.

One of England's greatest goalkeepers, Frank Swift retired at the age of 35, having played over 350 matches for Manchester City and over 30 Internationals (including war time) for England. Although certainly Manchester United tried to lure him out of his retirement, City would not let him go unless a transfer fee was paid. So Frank turned his hand to journalism, mainly with the News of the World.

Frank Swift was a big man, he lived his life to the full often being the man any crowd could appreciate with his sense of fun as he could make everybody laugh. A brilliant raconteur, in the dressing room his infectious good humour brought a smile to even the most nervous beginner. Whilst he was undoubtedly a showman, he was first and foremost a quite magnificent goalkeeper.

Whilst Matt Busby was a big friend of Frank Swift, there was one occasion when Matt wished Swifty had been miles away. That was a Scotland v England international played before a crowd in excess of 120,000 at

Hampden Park. England were actually leading 3-1 at the time but Scotland were getting well on top when they were awarded a penalty kick. Now both Matt and Frank practised daily for years so they both thought they could outwit the other as Matt stepped forward to try and bring his country back into the international. Which way to place it, right or left? Matt chose right, Frank guessed correctly and England survived the Scottish onslaught and won the match.

The Manchester United footballers just loved being around 'Big Swifty'. The journalists who were in Madrid for the European Cup first leg semi-final in 1957 were stood on the side of the pitch watching United train when Bobby Charlton, Billy Whelan and Dennis Viollet spotted Frank and pulled him onto the pitch so they could have their picture taken with him.

1958 started with Manchester United chasing a possible treble for the second successive season. In a handy position near the top of the League and a pivotal fixture against the leaders Wolverhampton Wanderers due at Old Trafford in early February, the team were also looking forward to the upcoming two legged tie against the excellent Yugoslav team Red Star Belgrade whilst the start of the FA Cup trail had paired them with an away fixture at Third Division (North) Workington Town. When the team went in at half time 1-0 down to Workington it was not looking good for the champions, bitterly cold and the pitch in a terrible icy, bumpy condition. As it turned out, a brilliant hat trick from Dennis Viollet put Manchester United into the 4th round with a 3-1 victory.

Frank Swift, writing in his weekly Sunday column for 'The News of the World' said; 'Dennis Viollet, Manchester United's goal poaching inside left, will remember this game for the rest of his life. His brilliantly taken hat trick in a dramatic six minutes saved his team from disaster. Dennis was superb. His balance and majestic control of the ball in such severe circumstances stamped him as a craftsman of the highest order.'

Such was the power of the press that, in the 1950's the News of the World would sell eight million copies of the paper on a Sunday, and Frank Swift was their leading sports columnist.

In the aftermath of the Red Star Belgrade match the team, officials and journalists all attended a banquet at the British Embassy in Belgrade, with Frank joining Bobby Charlton and Dennis Viollet in going off into what was a mild night in comparison to the teams arrival in Belgrade, in the company of some of the Embassy officials for a drink. Less than twenty four hours later, as Dennis Viollet was walking into the Rechts der Isar Hospital after his van journey from the shattering scene at the airport, the first person Dennis spotted was Frank Swift lying dead on a stretcher. Dennis passed out at the sight of a man he knew and admired so much. Frank had actually been alive when he had arrived at the hospital, but he died soon after whilst his injuries would have left him in a hopeless state had he survived.

Figure 23 Frank Swift Memorial Service & Memorabilia

Let Frank Swift's great friend Matt Busby pay his own tribute, *'I was with Big Swifty from his beginnings in league football with Manchester City. I would have signed him if I could for Manchester United, and I was with him when he died at Munich. He was only forty three. He died when he had so much fun still in him to share with friends, neighbours and strangers.'*

ERIC THOMPSON
'THE BLUE EYED COMEDIAN'

Figure 25 Eric Thompson

NO ONE SO 'MAD ABOUT SPORT' AS
—Eric Thompson

Figure 24 Daily Mail, February 7, 1958

As with all the journalists being discussed, Eric Thompson was a smart dresser, often sporting a dickey bow as his tie attire. Remember, as has been said a few times through this book, journalists were in many ways the voice of the people, putting out the information at the vanguard of that era's media.

Eric Thompson was somebody who kept people's spirits going in whatever the situation. A round faced, blue eyed man, he was the Daily Mail's sports writer who also combined being a cartoonist for the paper, often drawing sketches to illustrate his own articles. Well-liked by all who knew him, he seemed to have a quip or a joke at a stroke. A man who, seemingly, had no enemies, Eric Thompson was the smile on the face of gentleness, to him journalism was not a weapon but a thing of joy. He had been described by colleagues as the "J.B.Priestley of all Manchester's journalists, avuncular, a knowledgeable man and very wise. Having humour which was broader than J.B.Priestley and not nearly as acrid."

Figure 26 Matt Busby (United Review)

Eric was also an occasional guest contributor in United's matchday programme. In a programme against Sheffield United he wrote a very interesting article on collecting match programmes and photographs printed from the matches. Possibly one of the first articles on such a much loved collecting hobby. Certainly anyone that took his advice at the time would be grateful for his guidance. His drawings too, were featured in the programme. For example, Eric's portrait opposite was used to illustrate the 'Matt Busby Talking' column in the programme for the visit of Sunderland in April 1957. A portrait of Arthur Drewry, then F.A. Chairman and President of F.I.F.A. was included in the programme for the home leg of the semi-final against Real Madrid. In his accompanying article Eric titled United *'flying ambassadors'* as he reflected on the unifying nature of sport and the spirit behind what he called *'the globe-trotting game'*.

Eric had joined the Daily Mail in 1931 at the age of 21 and besides his

ARTHUR DREWRY

Figure 27 Arthur Drewry
(United Review)

detailed football analysis was an acknowledged expert on cricket and athletics as well. In all sports he gave the same quiet, thorough attention with acute analysis. Eric was the author of a bestselling book called, 'Mad about Sport', he was married with a step son who was in the Merchant Navy.

The Daily Mail replaced Eric Thompson as its Manchester football reporter with Gerald Williams, who in his later life would become a famous radio tennis commentator. Interestingly Williams himself had been recommended to the Daily Mail by his friend the famous boxing commentator Harry Carpenter.

CHAPTER TWO
PORTRAYAL OF THE BABES

Eight players died alongside the eight journalists at Munich. This chapter pays tribute to those players by providing pen portraits of the players taken from the reports written by the journalists at the time. The players are described in the order in which they made their debut.

MARK JONES

Figure 28 Mark Jones

Born: 15th June 1933, Barnsley.
Debut: 7 October 1950 v Sheffield Wednesday (H) League
Goals: 1
Appearances: 121
Position: Centre Half Back

Barnsley born Babe, Mark Jones was England Schoolboy captain and made his debut, at just 17, in 1950. Despite this early start, it was not until the 1954-55 season that he became a regular for the team. In part, this was due to the fact that early in 1953 he left to do his two years National service and he never figured in any first team games again until after his demobilization in early 1955. Writing in 1955 in his report of the home match against Wolverhampton Wanderers, Donny Davies made the point that Jones had taken time to settle, but was fulsome in his praise,:

'And above all they will applaud Mark Jones their young centre half-back whose impressive display against a centre forward of Swinbourne's class suggests that at last he is reaching fuller confidence and maturity.'

Centre-halfs are normally noted for their strength, rather than their skill. Nevertheless, Donny Davies saw beauty in his work:

'Wheeler's delightful artistry for Bolton was among the game's greatest pleasures, as was the beautiful defensive work of Jones.'

The Babes were, of course, renowned for their attacking prowess. In Europe though, there were times when solid defence was the order of the day. Mark Jones was a central character in these heroic battles. Dortmund away was a great example with Donny Davies and George Follows respectively describing his courageous contribution..

'Were one to apportion marks for outstanding individual, one would single out the respective centre half-backs, Michallek and Jones for major awards......Jones the Rock of Gibraltar.'

'Centre-half Mark Jones threw a mighty smokescreen in front of goalkeeper Wood'

The situation was repeated in the second-half of the final match in Belgrade. Mark Jones again central to a battling defensive display as Tom Jackson reported.

'Not a bit of it. Gregg, Foulkes, Mark Jones, and Roger Byrne never lost their heads in matching the Yugoslav forward.'

'But only three minutes remained for play, and Jones, Foulkes, Byrne. Edwards, and Colman, who had played magnificently throughout, saw to it that that goal never materialised.'

ROGER BYRNE

Figure 29 Roger Byrne

Born: 08 Feb 1929, Gorton.
Signed: 01 Mar 1949
Debut: 24 Nov 1951 v Liverpool (A) League
Goals: 20
Appearances: 280
Position: Full back

The leader of the Babes on and off the pitch, Roger Byrne made his debut aged 22 in the 0-0 draw at Anfield. Making his debut in the same match was 18 year old Jackie Blanchflower. The twin debuts are seen by some as the birth of the babes due to the headline of Tom Jackson's report in that night's Manchester Evening News, that read 'United's "babes" cool, confident'. In his report Jackson had this to say:

'It was a case of on with the old – and the new – at Anfield this afternoon, where Manchester United seeking their first victory this month, included four reserves against an unchanged Liverpool team.'

Byrne went on to become captain of the Babes and had the full respect of team-mates and journalists alike. Writing in the programme for the Babes' title winning victory over Blackpool Tom Jackson singled out his huge influence on the younger players:

'It has been a big strain for the young players in the side but Roger's leadership has been a feature in this tough going.'

Byrne's leadership was also praised by George Follows in the two legs against Borussia Dortmund. After describing him as 'refrigerator cool' in the home leg, Follows titled him 'Hero No. 1' in what he described as a rear-guard action, a match headlined with the telling title 'Byrne and his boys hang on for a place in the last 8.'

Byrne of course, was more than a leader. He was a highly talented full-back. Donny Davies summarised his abilities best, writing that Byrne was:

'......His usual swift, calculating, cool self. The other defenders worked hard, but they were drudges where Edwards and Byrne were artists.'

And on another occasion:

'Another player bent on distinguishing himself was Byrne. United's left-back Byrne's speed was remarkable, his tackling devastating: and it was something of a novelty for the Bolton crowd to see Holden, their own fleet-footed, outside-right, so repeatedly overtaken and robbed. To catch the eye as a defender, on a field that contained an Aston, a Carey, a Chilton, a Cockburn, a Wheeler, a Barass, and a Bell, all playing in a masterful vein was something of an achievement.'

DAVID PEGG

Figure 30 David Pegg

Born: 20th September 1935, Doncaster
Debut: 6th December 1952 v Middlesbrough (H) League
Goals: 24
Appearances: 127
Position: Outside Left

Doncaster born David Pegg was an ever present for United at outside left until competition for his place by Albert Scanlon.

As usual, Tom Jackson was on hand to see David Pegg score for United's 'A' Team on a historic occasion in Manchester.

"On Thursday night I was at The Cliff to see the first ever competitive fixture under those conditions (floodlights) *in Manchester. A crowd of 4,465 watched United's 'A' team play Leek Town in the Gilgryst Cup, which United won 3-2 with youngster David Pegg getting one of the goals."*

Still only 22 when he died, he was viewed by many as the natural successor to Tom Finney in the England side. Frank Swift's report of the 6-2 demolition of Arsenal at Old Trafford helps explain why:

'The magic boots of David Pegg flashed out an urgent message to the F.A. selectors at Old Trafford. Six times the net bulged and five times the move started with the tantalising left-winger. A Pegg corner brought Whelan's early equaliser to David Herd's fifth minute thunderbolt. Johnny Berry crashed home number 2 from a low Pegg centre a minute before a Pegg-Whelan short corner move allowed Edwards to do his best to burst the net with goal number three. The wriggling wraith had no part in the fourth goal… but the boy David pinpointed Tommy Taylor's head before it nodded the next one. And when Whelan completed the scoring with a right hook across the face of the goal, once again the ball had come from Pegg, via Taylor.'

As a member of the youth team Pegg had scored five goals in a record score of 23-0 against Nantwich which also included five goals from Duncan Edwards. As a result Pegg was elevated to the first team for his debut against Middlesbrough at Old Trafford. Incidentally, the week after Billy Foulkes was included for his debut away at Liverpool.

Donny Davies singled out Pegg in the 10-0 demolition of Anderlecht, with this memorable description of yet another headed goal by Tommy Taylor;

'Byrne cleared his lines with a superb volley and at the same time gave Pegg the sort of pass a winger dreams about. He ran off down the track round his man like an eel and dropped his centre just where Taylor wanted it. A leap, a downward header, a shower of raindrops from the goal net, and United were one up on the night. This sprightly left wing, with his deft ball control, his deceptive body swerves, and his choice of the right moment at which to part, was making a strong challenge to both Taylor and Colman as the finest player on the field. '

TOMMY TAYLOR

Figure 31 Tommy Taylor

Born: 29 Jan 1932, Barnsley.
Signed: 01 Mar 1953
Debut: 7 March 1953 v Preston (H) League
Goals: 131
Appearances: 191
Position: Forward

Tommy Taylor was famously brought to United for a fee of £29.999 so as to avoid the tag of a £30,000 player. United's centre-forward Taylor had an outstanding goal record and he was renowned for his aerial ability.

Writing of his debut in his inimitable fashion Donny Davies provides an outstanding summary of his talents:

'And what gave particular pleasure to the fine crowd enjoying the goal harvest and the spring sunshine was the manner in which young Taylor, from Barnsley, with the expert aid of Rowley and others, scored his first two goals for his new club. The first time Taylor breasted a high ball down to his feet and stroked it out to his wingman, a murmur of approval, like the sound of a wind rising, passed round the ground. "He'll do" exclaimed an old hand, removing his meerschaum for the purpose, "He's got it up here," he added, pointing sagely to own cranium. Certainly, from the point of view of tactical common sense as well as physical proportions Taylor seems ideally equipped. He stands just over six feet in height, has the clean trim appearance of, say, the Australian (Keith) Miller, the same powerful set of shoulders, and can ride easily any but the heaviest charges. Moreover, he has springs in his heels and can use his head to telling effect. He had already given proof of this by rising to Pegg's floating corner-kick and steering it narrowly wide of the post, and this persuaded Rowley that the time was ripe for better things. Tearing after a cunning pass by Carey, Rowley gave one swift glance inwards, then swept a model centre as only he can across Taylor's path. Taylor leapt like a trout to a fly and a glorious header whizzed between the posts. '

Other reporters were less expansive in their assessments but equally respectful, George Fellows describing Taylor as *'A one man forward line'* and

Eric Thompson praising his work rate, saying that he was *'Always full of great-hearted dash'.*

The exception to this unanimity of opinion was provided by Henry Rose. Always happy to court controversy, Rose famously stated that *'if Taylor was the best centre forward in England, he was Father Christmas.'* It is the mark of both men that, despite this, they became friends. Indeed Rose and Taylor could be seen chatting happily together on the journey to Belgrade

Perhaps Taylor's greatest game was as the star of what many consider United's greatest ever match - the 3-0 victory over Bilbao at Maine Road. In the build up to the game Bilbao's Jesus Garay was lauded as Europe's number one centre-half. On the night there was only one winner of the personal duel between the two. The Manchester Evening News collated the press reports from all of the journalists there that night. They all came to the same conclusion that headed the article- *'Fantastic Game and Taylor Tops!'*

DUNCAN EDWARDS

Figure 32 Duncan Edwards

Born: 01 Oct 1936, Dudley
Debut: 04 April 1953 v Cardiff (H) League
Goals total: 21
Appearances: 177
Position: Half-back

Duncan Edwards, above all others, symbolises the team known as the Busby Babes. Acknowledged by all his teammates, opponents, fans and journalists alike, as one of the greatest there will ever be.

Duncan's ability and reputation within the club were such that his debut was eagerly anticipated. Tom Jackson first mentioned Duncan in the programme in 1952, stating that *'last week I saw the start of what seems to be the start of a very promising Manchester United career as Duncan Edwards made his debut in a United shirt in the Public Practice match at Old Trafford'*

Alf Clarke later wrote: *'We cannot escape the fact that Duncan Edwards is the greatest young player of his age. I know we have had the Bastin's, Carter's, Doherty's and others but I rank Edwards as the best young player I have ever seen. He is a future England captain.*

'Edwards, as big as a tank and as tough as Wilf Copping, is the greatest of England's post war finds.'

Eric Thompson also emphasised his strength: *'Muscular Duncan Edwards bulldozed his way forward and slipped a perfect pass to Scanlon...... always a powerful, roaming, indefatigable figure. He often pushed past two or three challenges to swing passes to Pegg'.*

George Follows memorably described Edwards scoring for England:

'Went through like a tank in the 28th minute, destroying four tackles and bashed in the goal that he had been threatening to bash in throughout the tour.'

More insight into life as player at that time is provided by the excellent 3 part article in October 1957's Daily Mirror by Archie Ledbrooke and Frank McGhee. Focussing on Duncan they were unable to hide their admiration of his journey at United since his signature at fifteen and a half:

'He had hopes and ambitions and dreams. THEY ALL CAME TRUE. He was twenty just a few days ago. Now he has ten full international caps, a League championship medal and other trifles including three FA Youth Cup medals. He is still a boy, one of hundreds of thousands still in khaki. His National Service does not end until next May. But already he is world famous. HE IS DUNCAN EDWARDS. He is quoted everywhere as the ultimate end product of the United system which has written a new phrase into the dictionary of football: The Busby Babes.'

His reputation continued to grow. Writing in 1957 about United's 2-0 victory over Birmingham City, Archie Ledbrooke put it this way:

'Edwards is the one that set the pattern. He is the footballer of the year. He is the footballer of almost any year. He could be given England's captaincy NOW and carry it lightly on those giant shoulders.'

GEOFF BENT

Figure 33 Geoff Bent

Born: 27th September 1932, Irlams O' Th' Height, Salford
Debut: 20th February 1954 v Burnley (A) League
Goals: 0
Appearances: 12
Position: Full Back

Local lad Geoff Bent was a squad player for Manchester United, in an era before the term had been coined. In fact, United's strength in depth was a big part of their success at this time, with quality replacements in every position, ready to step up to the mark if an injury hit a first team player. As Roger Byrne's understudy, Geoff Bent's appearances were only ever likely to be sporadic. Nevertheless, he was a first class player in his own right and considered by all to be an able deputy for Byrne. There was a danger that Byrne might have to miss the Red Star game through injury and so Geoff Bent made the fateful trip.

Earlier in his career Donny Davies had spotted his potential, remarking:

'For the heroes of their pulse stirring recovery, the winners will turn less fervently to their forward line than to their defenders. To plucky little Whitefoot, for instance at right-half, where his nagging interventions did so much to disturb Willshaw's poise: or to Bent; their newest discovery at left back, and a shrewd tactician in the making. Bent's watchful

surveillance over the perky, ebullient Hancocks was a telling factor in United's success.'

Remarking on the strength of the squad that United took to Red Star Donny Davies pointed out that of the six 'reserve' players that had travelled, five were full internationals, he then said:

The sixth, Bent, though without a cap, is nevertheless known to be a first class substitute for Byrne.

As a local boy and a fan, Bent was proud simply to get the chance to play for United having joined the ground staff as early as 1948. On the M.U.S.T. webpages Tom Clare recounts that Bent's proudest moment came when he faced Tom Finney. .

'Probably THE highlight of his career (in his own view anyway) was taking the ball off the legendary Tom Finney in a game. He treasured the newspaper cutting of the event he valued so much. I think that it is simultaneously wonderfully poignant and yet carries in it the joy of a footballer who was also a huge fan of the games finest.'

LIAM WHELAN

Figure 34 Liam 'Billy' Whelan

Born: 1st April 1935, Dublin
Debut: 26th March 1955 v Preston North End (a) League
Goals: 52
Appearances: 98
Position: Inside Right

Liam 'Billy' Whelan is one of a long line of Irish United players that came to the club from Dublin's Home Farm. A ball playing inside-right with a fantastic scoring record – he was the club's top scorer in 1956-57, in what Henry Rose described as a *'whale of a season' for him,* when he scored 33 goals in total with 27 in the league.

Henry went on to describe him as a *'broth of a boy'* after he notched a goal for United in their 5-3 defeat at Bilbao. *'British hearts are high here tonight, and the man who is responsible for that is a broth of a boy from Dublin, 21 year old Bill Whelan.'*

Liam was a definite favourite of Donny Davies, who seemed to be enthralled by the combination of his laconic manner coupled with magical skills. Describing him memorably as the *'blandest and daintiest of the present day masters of surprise.'*

In an international between Ireland and England, Liam had the opportunity to pit his wits against his teammates Duncan Edwards & Roger Byrne. Donny Davies described the battle:

'Whelan demonstrated his subtle ball play at its best, much to Edwards discomfiture.... the skill of the Irish in general and of Whelan in particular completely dominated the scene........eventually Whelan produced an example of inside forward play

fit for the Hibernian Museum. He first rendered Byrne innocuous with a perfect scooped pass to Ringstead and then ran in to receive Ringstead's equally beautiful square pass in return.'

In a match at home to Arsenal, Edwards was glad to have the *'bland'* Whelan back as a team-mate:

'Whelan decided now that the type of football served up, rich as it was by now, would be all the better with a little Irish flavouring. Taking a short corner kick from Pegg and mesmerising an opponent (by a superb dummy) into dashing wildly in the wrong direction. Whelan then blandly tapped the ball back to Taylor so neatly that though Taylor's shot dug into somebody's ribs and bounced back Edwards had time to hurl himself at the rebound and fill the Arsenal goalmouth with the dust from a monstrous and explosive shot.'

Wolves at home provided another opportunity for Donny Davies to describe the Irishman's talents:

'By general consent the prize for the most laughs this week must go to Whelan —the thin wisp of an Irishman who plays inside right, with a few variations of his own, for United. His first goal was characteristic. Affecting to let a pass from Charlton run on to someone else, he suddenly trod on the ball, gazing blandly round as who should say "Anybody any objections?" before producing from his frail drumstick legs-a violent-scoring shot fit to tear the net away. From that point onwards his ball control, exhibited with a deceptive air of casualness and unconcern, with occasional lapses into pure waggishness, kept the stands and terraces bubbling with delight.'

EDDIE COLMAN

Figure 35 Eddie Colman

Born: 01 Nov 1936, Salford
Debut: 12 Nov 1955 v Bolton (A) League
Goals: 2
Appearances: 108
Position: Half back

Eddie "Snakehips" Colman was a local lad. A crowd-pleasing half-back in a team of crowd pleasers. He was full of raw ability, but according to Jimmy Murphy in this interview with Archie Ledbrooke & Frank McGhee, it was a talent that had to be carefully honed:

'Anyone can spot a Duncan Edwards. The true art of scouting is to see something the others have missed." We can cite the case of Eddie Colman, currently starring at right half in the first team and probably the finest uncapped player in the country. Eddie was not a schoolboy international, like so many brilliant United youngsters. Other clubs were not interested in him. He was under-sized. His football was all wrong. He persisted in holding the ball rather than passing. "But we saw something in him," says Murphy. "So we signed him . . . and then had to reverse all his natural football instincts"'

Murphy's instinct (as always) was proved right. Once established, he was an ever present for United. Old International described his snake hips this way as he reported on the 10-0 demolition of Anderlecht in 1956

'Colman… with his amusing "shimmy shakes" and body wiggles'. Henry Rose was briefer but just as memorable describing it as a *'Monroe wriggle'.* He was more than a showman though – he was a brilliantly effective player for United. This report describing Eddie at his finest, is also Donny Davies at his brilliant enjoyable but effective best.

The feature of the first half was a brilliant display by Colman. Never has this gifted young half-back intervened more cleverly, used the ball more wisely, or sold his dummies more shyly, than in this instance. He had on the other side, a formidable rival by the name of Scoular; himself a strong tackler, a wise distributor, and a subtle tactician in the Newcastle interest, and one who was plainly determined to leave his mark, if not on the players, at any rate on the proceedings. It is to Scoular's credit that in spite of the overwhelming odds, against him, he like his goalkeeper, Simpson, left the field at the close with his reputation if anything slightly enhanced But in comparison with Colman's joyous and effective artistry Scoular's work, though telling seemed heavy and laboured. Colman might have been the "premier danseur" in a Footballers' Ballet and Scoular the dogged leader of a Chain Gang. One of these days, perhaps, when Colman is in the mood, we shall have the Beswick Prize Band accompanying him with snatches of reasonably tuneful ballet music—say from Swan Lake. Then we shall see the little fellow at his best.'

CHAPTER THREE
THE BIRTH OF THE BABES

The birth of the Busby Babes can be traced back to the moment that Matt Busby was appointed manager of Manchester United on October 22, 1945. As competitive football returned after the Second World War the size of the task facing Busby was huge. Old Trafford had been blitzed during the Second World War, and they had to reconstruct with players resuming their careers after the deprivation of war. The players' adaptations were also echoed by the journalists of the time who had also suffered during the six-year period of war time action, as had the public of course. All were hungry for the simple pleasures of life and the sense of community that football brought to them.

While Busby was new to the club, many of the people around him had a long history at United. Two men in particular had been documenting the rise and fall of United in the programme at every home match since the thirties. The first ever edition of the programme which became synonymous with Manchester United, the 'United Review' was produced for the Division Two match against Stoke City on August 27, 1932.

The main contributors were Alf Clarke and Tom Jackson of the Manchester Evening Chronicle and the Manchester Evening News respectively. They would feature in the programme until the dreadful air crash in Munich on February 6, 1958 under the headings Alf's 'Casual Comments' and Tom's 'Tom Jackson Talks' page. Tom also gave a review of the players who would feature in the opposition team as well. Their last articles were actually in the February 8 edition printed for the forthcoming Saturday match against Wolverhampton Wanderers. All copies of that were ordered to be destroyed immediately after the crash, but it is believed a handful did survive and now fetch very high sums if they are ever sold in auctions.

The programme was restored to its former glory for the first game after the Second World War against Grimsby Town, a First Division fixture played on August 31, 1946 but at Maine Road, home of Manchester City as Old Trafford was still undergoing repair work after its devastating bomb damage in the early 1940's. In the programme Alf Clarke recalled the last League fixture Manchester United had played on the Saturday, a day before the outbreak of the war, a match at The Valley against Charlton Athletic.

'We had reached Euston Station on the Friday night. All street lighting was extinguished. Searchlights played around in the sky. Come the dawn, we went to Charlton, barrage balloons were flying around the ground. The atmosphere was electric, but football was not the public fancy at that moment. If I remember rightly, about 5,000 turned up to see Charlton win 2-0 with Allenby Chilton making his United debut but minds were far away fearing the future.'

Meanwhile, Tom Jackson wrote of a match Manchester United had played in Hamburg against the B.A.O.R. (British Army of the Rhine) when flying arrangements to get the team back to play a match at Bradford had broken down.

"The Army authorities hustled to some effect to ensure a special coach, normally reserved for high ranking officers (nothing less than Colonels), was put at their disposal on the rail trip to Calais, with all the players having sleeping compartments. Imagine the surprise the following morning for the Brigadiers, Major Generals etc when the United team walked into their dining coach for breakfast!"

The articles set the scene perfectly into which the Babes would eventually emerge. The privations of the war and a country where footballers, although much loved, were still ordinary working people. Nowadays the roles would be reversed with Brigadiers only able to dream of the life and luxury of a footballer.

Despite inheriting a situation with so many immediate difficulties to be overcome, Sir Matt had a long-term plan and was determined to put it into place. Archie Ledbrooke wrote that Busby's first public words as manager were as follows:

'I am determined that Manchester United shall provide the great football public of Manchester with the best possible in the game. IT IS MY INTENTION TO DEVELOP YOUNG PLAYERS.'

That statement has proven to be remarkably prophetic. The team's rise to the top was achieved by the disciplined execution of that plan over the coming years. Indeed, it is a plan that was followed by Sir Alex Ferguson and, for many, characterises United to this day some 70 years later.

Times were tough, but the return of football after the war brought huge interest as people had been starved of competitive football for seven years, and crowds regularly exceeding 60,000 were seen. While Busby had his plan to put his faith in youth, others weren't so patient. Along with the big crowds came revenue of course and Tom Jackson commented in the programme against Chelsea on the high transfer fee paid by Liverpool for Newcastle United's Albert Stubbins.

'This deal which was for £13,000 brought raised eyebrows as being an awful lot of money to spend on one player when the game of football relied so much on team work.'

United needed money of course to rebuild the stadium, and when Brentford arrived at Maine Road, Tom Jackson continued the theme of high crowds and money coming into the game by speculating on the 'new' Old Trafford. 'I hear that discussions are being had about the capacity of Old Trafford when it finally gets rebuilt, with comments that perhaps the attendance could be increased to 125,000 when building materials become more readily available.'

Despite playing their fixtures at Maine Road in the first season after the war, 1946-47, United were runners up in the League. This was built on in 1948, a season which would see Manchester United win the FA Cup for only the second time in their history, while still playing their home fixtures at Maine Road. When United received a couple of 'home' draws in the cup they had to play them away from Maine Road as City were also drawn at home! So, Liverpool had to be played across their city at Everton's Goodison Park then Charlton Athletic had to be played at Huddersfield Town's Leeds Road ground. When, finally, United could play a 'home' tie against Preston North End in the sixth round Alf Clarke was keen to appraise United fans of one of the Preston players. A player born within miles of Matt Busby that also went on to be one of football's legends as manager of Liverpool.

"I would urge all young footballers to keep their eyes on the Preston wing half today who is a credit to the game. His name? Bill Shankly."

The football played by the team of this era saw Busby deliver against the first part of his promise to provide the public of Manchester with the best. The team were famous for their fast passing and movement and in the words of Alec Sharrocks were rightly hailed as 'Winners & Champions'. Donny Davies made full use of the opportunity afforded by an extensive Cup Final report to display his talents:

Figure 36 Manchester Guardian, April 26, 1948

'Quietly, and with what Fabian called the "inevitability of gradualness" Manchester United twice were in arrears, twice caught up again, and then beat Blackpool in the final of the FA Cup competition at Wembley Stadium by four goals to two.'

'If Carey had crossed a gypsy's palm with silver and been told "You'll have a mort of trouble from two blond players at the start, but don't worry – all will come right in the end." You could scarcely have expected a more curious air of unconcern and detachment.'

Reporting a disputed penalty decision, he wrote:

'Only Sam Weller's double million magnifying glass of hextry power could have settled the doubt if it had occurred inches inside or inches outside of "the box".'

Finally, he observed that:

'When the match was over the Blackpool players deliberately stood apart so that Manchester United should have all the glory, and led the crowd's applause. A fine gesture, that for a team which twice had the cup within its grasp and saw it slip; one that symbolised neatly the warm regard in which Manchester United were held.'

The report is typical of the much-loved style of The Old International. It combines a knowledge of history (Fabian) and literature (Dickens, Sam Weller), but in a manner, though enjoyable in its own right, truly captured the spirit of the game.

During the 1948-49 season news finally came that Manchester United would finally be able to return home for the start of the following season. Alf Clarke gave details in his programme notes.

"What great news that United can finally return home next season! Whilst parts of the Old Trafford stadium will still be under a rebuild, and there will be no covered areas,

the attendance will be limited to 60,000 of which 3,000 cinema type seats will be available."

And so 'Back Home' was blazed across the cover of the first programme for the first match back at Old Trafford in 1949 against Bolton Wanderers with Alf Clarke being himself in the news. Alf was congratulated on the start of his twenty sixth season with the club, reporting in the programme and in his day job at the Manchester Evening Chronicle. Alf himself said: *"Those twenty six years have seen the joy of winning the FA Cup but also the rescue victory avoiding relegation to the Third Division in the mid 1930's by beating Millwall 2-0."*

Much work was being done in the background at that time. Tom Jackson in the programme for the visit of Middlesbrough devoted a full page to what was happening in the restructure of the club right down to the youth level in which both Matt Busby and Jimmy Murphy placed such importance.

"The M.U.J.A.C. organisation, or to give it its full title of Manchester United Junior Athletic Club, is going from strength to strength since the war. Although started prior to that, now the grounding the young players of the future has to go through is under chief coach Jimmy Murphy and his assistant Bert Whalley on a Tuesday and a Thursday night at The Cliff, the United training ground in Salford, where all the facets of professional football was explained to the young hopefuls, of whom Dennis Viollet, Mark Jones and Jackie Blanchflower were showing their paces this season."

Those three, of course, would become bedrocks of the team to be known as the 'Busby Babes' and indeed, the first member of that side would make his debut against Newcastle United this season, goalkeeper Ray Wood who had signed from Darlington and played against another North-East side, Newcastle United.

The ever changing face of football was mentioned by Tom Jackson in his notes for the visit of Blackpool. United had toured America in the close season and Tom spoke of what had really impressed Matt Busby whilst over there,

"Both Matt Busby and John Carey had their eyes open, literally, at the sight of floodlight football. They both firmly believed that it would revolutionise the whole sporting scene in our country if introduced."

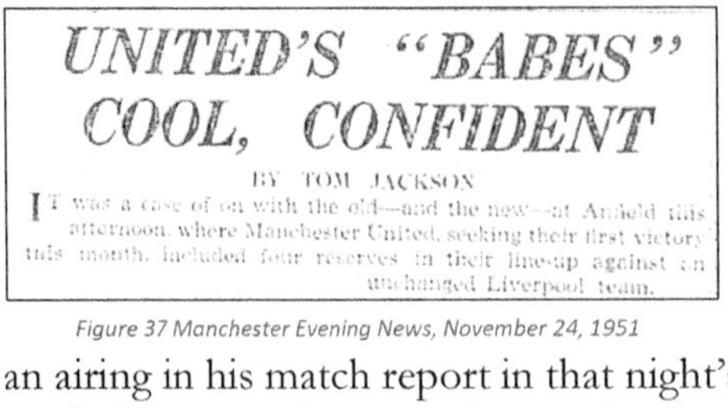

UNITED'S "BABES" COOL, CONFIDENT

BY TOM JACKSON

IT was a case of on with the old—and the new—at Anfield this afternoon, where Manchester United, seeking their first victory this month, included four reserves in their line-up against an unchanged Liverpool team.

Figure 37 Manchester Evening News, November 24, 1951

In November 1951 two more of what was to be a great future for Manchester United made their debuts in the match at Liverpool. Roger Byrne (21) and Jackie Blanchflower(18) helped Tom Jackson give the tag 'Babes' an airing in his match report in that night's newspaper. During the following week, Tom was also reporting on the floodlights that had so impressed Matt Busby and Johnny Carey the previous year in America.

Not all the players came through the youth system though. Alf Clarke reported on a very important signing for Manchester United.

"Following the departure of Jimmy Delaney, Manchester United obviously needed a quality outside right and it looks as though they may have found him. I was at Manchester London Road Station (now Manchester Piccadilly) waiting to meet Johnny Berry who had just been signed from Birmingham City. Berry had played an excellent match last year when Birmingham had knocked United out of the cup. Whilst waiting for a new star outside right for United I bumped into an old favourite in that position, Joe Spence. Joe had coined one of the famous sayings, 'Give it to Joe'."

Although starting the following season as league champions, 1952-53 was to become a transitional period with the breakup of the 1948 cup winning side and the past season's title winners and the formation of the Busby Babes' continuing. In the first programme of the season Tom Jackson gave further news of this transition.

"It has been such a quiet season transfer wise in football that I wonder if the days of the 'Bank of England' transfer deals have ended. Mind you, last week I saw the start of what seems to be the start of a very promising Manchester United career as Duncan Edwards made his debut in a United shirt in the Public Practice match at Old Trafford. Duncan was last season's England Schoolboy Captain and left half and hails from Dudley"

The presence of players such as Duncan Edwards convinced Matt Busby that his plan was beginning to bear fruit. Although the team was in a transitional state, Alf Clarke was able to report from Matt Busby's message at a recent shareholder's meeting, with hindsight these were truly prophetic words.

"Whilst Matt Busby was, naturally, delighted with the senior team winning the league the previous season, he also mentioned that in his opinion the young players on the Manchester United books were worth hundreds of thousands of pounds. In a couple of years' time we shall have some wonderful material when needed most"

If proof was needed to support Matt's confidence the start of the FA Youth Cup that month provided solid evidence. Manchester United were in a perfect position to start it. A record score of 23-0 against Nantwich (which still stands) included five goals apiece from David Pegg and Duncan Edwards, with Pegg being elevated, alongside Billy Foulkes, to a first team debut at Liverpool. Later In the season, a major signing by Matt Busby of Tommy Taylor for £29,999 from Barnsley signified his desire to complete a side that would be young, hungry and able to win trophies.

The elevation to the first team from joining the club as a junior at the start of the season was complete for Duncan Edwards when he was thrust into action against Cardiff City on the 4th April 1953. A remarkable rise for what would turn out to be a remarkable footballer. Tom Jackson reported in the Manchester Evening News how Duncan had been given the news that he was to make his debut.

Edwards, 16, in United's first team

BY TOM JACKSON

DUNCAN EDWARDS, aged 16, reported at Manchester United's headquarters at Old Trafford to-day for duty as usual with the ground staff—and a few minutes later received the biggest news of his life. He was told by Mr. Matt Busby; "Go and get your football boots, son, you're playing for the first team against Cardiff City."

Figure 38 Manchester Evening News, April 23, 1953

'DUNCAN EDWARDS, aged 16, reported at Manchester United's headquarters at Old Trafford today for duty as usual with the ground staff—and a few minutes later received the biggest news of his life. He was told by Mr. Matt Busby: "Go and get your football boots, son, you're playing for the first team against Cardiff City." Though thrilled by the news Edwards took it calmly, he asked permission to 'phone his parents at Dudley, Worcestershire, and then raced a few hundred yards to give "Ma Watson, the landlady who looks after him and several other Busby youngsters, the big tidings.'

The report provides a marvellous insight into Duncan, and the life of a young footballer at that time. On the one hand destined for greatness and about to make your debut, on the other just a normal 16 year-old boy phoning his parents and sharing the news with his beloved landlady.

A week after this game, Dennis Viollet was given his debut, so for what would be regarded as the normal 'Busby Babes' line up in the future, nine players had now played for the club, in Wood, Foulkes, Byrne, Jones, Edwards, Berry, Taylor, Viollet and Pegg.

The following season (1953-54) would see these players truly emerge as a force. Writing in his 'Soccer Secrets' column before the start of that season George Follows reported with remarkable foresight:

'.....about Busby there is a bloom and a sparkle that has nothing to do with the steaks and sunshine of his summer stay in the USA. He has glowed gently with concealed lighting ever since the night of May 4 when his under-18 team walloped the young Wolves 7-1 to become undisputed youth champions. "That", he says, "is the finest display that I saw by any team last season".

Matt as ever was a man of patience. Follows reported that there were a full range of young players knocking at the door, including Duncan Edwards, described by Busby as 'The finest 16 year old I've ever seen'. Even so, although he was expecting a good season better was to come and Follows wrote 'it is in 1955 that he (Busby) expects the full changeover from veterans to youth'.

Pearson, Rowley out of United XI

Figure 39 Manchester Evening Chronicle, October 29, 1953

It was in a friendly in Scotland that the line-up recognisable as the Busby Babes first played together. On Wednesday the 28th October 1953 United played Kilmarnock in a friendly match to mark the unofficial launch of the floodlights at Rugby Park. As usual Alf Clarke was there to report that both Pearson and Rowley were carrying slight knocks and were to be replaced by Jackie Blanchflower and Dennis Viollet. In his match report the following day Clarke reported that Henry Cockburn the scorer of the opening goal in a 3-0 victory for United had to be substituted by Duncan Edwards in the 10th minute after breaking his jaw. Viollet and Taylor scored the other two goals. Edwards had played one match previously (against Cardiff) but the injury to Cockburn together with the manner of the victory over Kilmarnock made it highly likely that Edwards would retain his place for the league match on Saturday at Huddersfield.

Busby's Bouncing Babes
Keep All Town Awake!

Figure 40 Football Pink, April 28, 1953

MANCHESTER UNITED. — Wood; Foulkes Byrne; Whitefoot, Chilton, Edwards; Berry, Blanchflower, Taylor, Viollet, Rowley.

Edwards did indeed retain his place at Huddersfield as did Blanchflower and Viollet. Ray Woods and Bill Foulkes also came into the team having been unavailable for the midweek match due to army duties. In his match report for the Manchester Evening Chronicle Alf Clarke stated that *'the accent was on youth for the Manchester United team'*. More famously still the headline to his report in the 'Pink' that evening had the now famous headline above.

Both Alf Clarke and Tom Jackson had views on the youth policy sweeping Manchester United in 1954 in the programme for the visit of Bolton Wanderers, Alf commented, *"Matt Busby was a very proud man last week when he travelled to Italy to see Duncan Edwards, Ray Wood and Jeff Whitefoot play for England U23 team against their Italian equivalent, with Billy Foulkes and Dennis Viollet being travelling reserves. Manchester United now have one of the youngest ever First Division sides with an average age of under 21."* In the same programme Tom Jackson recalled earlier times, *"It is great to see all these younger players getting their chance with Manchester United, I can recall when John Carey, Stan Pearson and Jack Rowley all made their debuts in 1937/38 season."*

Stan Pearson was the subject of Alf Clarke's comments when Tottenham Hotspur came to Old Trafford, *"After seventeen years marvellous service and 450 appearances to Manchester United, Stan Pearson has decided to finish his career at Bury."* Included in the Tottenham side were two future great managers, Bill Nicholson who would lead Tottenham to the elusive double of League and Cup winners a few years later, and Alf Ramsey who would lead England to their only World Cup triumph in 1966.

Football today exists in inflationary times, telephone number transfer dealings and subsequent losses by football clubs, Alf Clarke's comments therefore in the programme for the visit of Sheffield Wednesday sixty years or so ago makes enlightening reading today. "Manchester United reported their balance sheet recently which showed a profit of over £19,000, which brought the overall profit in the post war years to £250,000."

Although totally inconceivable now, back in the 1950's international matches were played on a Saturday with the League campaign running alongside of them. Tom Jackson felt this was a massive reason for United's defeat the previous week at Wolverhampton Wanderers as he explained for the visit of Cardiff City.

'Last week's international in Belfast between Northern Ireland and England was a great testimony to the current Manchester United side as Ray Wood, Billy Foulkes, and Roger Byrne represented England and Jackie Blanchflower Northern Ireland. The down side was that the performance at Wolves was affected by the player changes, although congratulations to Ian Greaves who made his United debut.'

That defeat though was only a blip, as by the visit of Newcastle United all the club's sides were flying high as Alf Clarke reported. *"The various league tables make good reading for all 'red' fans with the first team top of the league, the reserves in second place and all the junior sides top of their respectively tables. Whilst I was in London last week with the United team who recorded an amazing 6-5 victory at Chelsea, I met up with Mr Bela P. Miklos who acts as interpreter for British teams abroad."*

Couple of points from this Newcastle match, Mr Miklos would, sadly, be one of those killed in the Munich air disaster, whilst Bobby Charlton's uncle, Jackie Milburn was in the Newcastle side on the day Bobby scored six goals for United's 'A' team against Accrington Stanley reserves.

Manchester United's young side could not hold their pace after Christmas, mind you a FA Cup exit at Maine Road to City and then a 5-0 hammering by the same team, only this time at Old Trafford did not help matters! Alf Clarke was always regarded as bleeding a United red blood but one of the directors at the time, Dr W. MacLaren was even more so, remarking to Alf after the 5-0 City defeat, "I saw two bad sides out there today Alf!"

By the time Sheffield United came to Old Trafford late in the season, both Alf Clarke and Tom Jackson reflected on old and new Manchester United heroes. Alf Clarke was discussing Duncan Edwards, *"Duncan making his England debut today against Scotland at Wembley Stadium is a marvellous tribute to the young man, who was first seen in the Public Practice match at the start of last season."* Tom Jackson was discussing a player at the other end of his career, *"Allenby Chilton's departure from Old Trafford to take up the player manager role at Grimsby Town ends eighteen years great service for Manchester United as captain, cup and league winner."*

CHELSEA'S VISIT TO OLD TRAFFORD
By an Old International
Manchester United 2, Chelsea 1   were soon hurling themselves at the

Figure 41 Manchester Guardian, April 30, 1955

The last match of this season saw United complete a league double over the side who would be champions, Chelsea. As Busby had predicted to George Follows the changeover was, indeed, completed in 1955. Donny Davies described, what now seems like a ceremonial changing of the guard. The United team gave the champions a guard of honour and the United fans there that day gave them an *'ovation fit for Genghis Khan or Tamerlane'* but there was no sentimentality in what followed, as Chelsea *'proceeded to get their noses rubbed well into the dust for the second time this season by a set of youngsters whose ideas they still cannot rumble.*

44

Co-Author Roy Cavanagh was also at that game. It is one he has particularly vivid memories of.

'I recall going to the match at Old Trafford with my late father Albert who introduced me to both football and cricket. United had won an incredible game at Stamford Bridge 6-5 and won this last match 2-1 as they were putting themselves to be the heir apparent for the title. One moment after this game I never forgot was my dad taking my autograph book and actually getting on the Chelsea coach for them all to sign. The problem was the coach drove off up the forecourt with my dad on it! Thankfully, it stopped at the top road and he gave me a book full of the champion's signatures.'

The next two seasons saw the Busby Babes dominate and indeed no English team were able to rumble this set of youngsters' ideas!

CHAPTER FOUR
DOMINATION AT HOME

The 1955-56 season marked the beginning of the Busby Babes' domination of domestic football. Pre-season the club had toured Scandinavia as Alf Clarke reported in the opening home match programme against Tottenham Hotspur,

'A very successful tour of Scandinavia resulted in four victories for the team, as the young players showed they were adaptable for all types of the game.'

It wasn't all plain sailing though and the season did not start well. In September 1955 United lost three of their six games. It was clear that the team, despite their talent, had a lot to learn.

As they entered October they were in need of a change of fortune. The home match against Wolves marked consecutive home victories. It demonstrated the teams fighting spirit as they came back from 2-1 and 3-2 down to win 4-3 in the dying seconds. As ever Donny Davies captured the day perfectly, describing the roar that greeted United's winning goal.

Association Football
OLD TRAFFORD'S ROARING DAY
Tables Turned on Wolverhampton
BY AN OLD INTERNATIONAL

Figure 42 Manchester Guardian, October 8, 1955

'To the accompaniment of a roar that must: have turned the lions at Belle Vue green with envy, and by railing on the last reserves of their spirit and energy when all seemed lost, Manchester United snatched a dramatic 4-3 victory over Wolverhampton Wanderers at Old Trafford on Saturday in the `dying moments of a tense swaying struggle whose frank hard-hitting and hell-for-leather slogging appealed more perhaps to the emotions than to the intellect.'

Although the side had started the season in mixed form, by November they were closing in at the top of the table. Roy Cavanagh recalls being at Burnden Park, then home of Bolton Wanderers, when local Salford lad Eddie Colman made his debut for United, being the last of what were the well-remembered regular side of the 'Busby Babes', Wood, Foulkes, Byrne (capt), Colman, Jones, Edwards, Berry, Whelan, Taylor, Viollet and Pegg, to make the first team. *"My father and I went by local coach firm Fieldsends, a journey which is about ten miles but seemed to take hours! We queued on the large forecourt, most games pay at the door in those days, before getting in after five minutes had been played and United were already one up thanks to a Tommy Taylor goal. What really impressed me though was that I was stood next to this enormous floodlight pylon, the first one I had ever seen, this 1955, Old Trafford would be March 1957 before their's opened. Sadly, Bolton finished up 3-1 winners but I had seen a lad who lived near me in Ordsall make his Manchester United debut and seen floodlights in operation!"*

Tom Jackson mentioned the Bolton match in the programme for next week's visit of Chelsea.

'Despite losing at Bolton, the debut of Eddie Colman was a great success. Today last season champions Chelsea come to Old Trafford with an unwelcome record for London clubs who have played 38 times at Old Trafford since one won here.'

This game made it 39 as United won 3-0.

As Easter approached Manchester United were firmly at the top of the league, whilst Tom Jackson informed of another parting former star in the Cardiff City match programme. *'John Aston was a great player in quite a few positions for Manchester United. The fact that the club is awarding him a testimonial at the end of the season is a reflection of his great service to the club.'*

By early April the confirmation of Manchester United as champions would be secured if they beat second placed Blackpool at Old Trafford. In the programme for that game Alf Clarke and Tom Jackson were full of information. Alf Clarke in his 'Casual Comments':

'From being top of the table on December 17, Manchester United have negotiated a long and difficult road, but today are set to be crowned as champions of England. Three of the side are likely to be in the England team to play Scotland at Hampden Park next week when United will be away at Sunderland. It is not just the first team who are successful though as the reserves are running away with their title, especially after beating Chesterfield 8-0 last week when young Bobby Charlton scored six of the goals. Bobby is also the leading light in this season's FA Youth Cup side who are again in the semi-final of that competition.'

Tom Jackson in his 'United Topics' was also, of course, very complementary on the team's performance, and about the captaincy of Roger Byrne.

'It has been a big strain for the young players in the side but Roger's leadership has been a feature in this tough going.'

Roy Cavanagh was fortunate to get a late invite to the match. Something that would be unimaginable now in the days when matches are almost always all ticket.

'I remember the match vividly as my Uncle Tom came around about 12.30 and asked if I fanied going to the game. Did I want to go? You bet! My late father Albert, had been a prisoner of war with the Japanese and suffered badly so it was difficult for him to take me some times to the games but this was one I wanted to see badly.

Off we went, crossing the Trafford Road swing bridge, buying the programme before you got to the ground. Very few all ticket matches those days except for seating areas, so searching for open turnstiles was our first problem. Many had already been closed nearly two hours before kick-off, until finally, at the big open Stretford End we managed to get in. That might have been the first achievement, the second was impossible for a little nine year old, as we struggled up the many steps to reach the top of the, then, still fully uncovered Stretford End. All that welcomed us was the many back ends of people already struggling to see what was happening on the pitch. For my part it was impossible, so I turned round and hey, on the back of Old Trafford in those days was the football pitch of Glovers Cables and they had a match on!"

Association Football

OLD TRAFFORD'S GREAT DAY

Blackpool's Challenge Stoutly Met

BY AN OLD INTERNATIONAL

Figure 43 Manchester Guardian, April 7, 1956

Donny Davies had a better view and saw Manchester United come from a goal behind to beat Blackpool 2-1 and win the First Division title for the first time with this young side. He provided a classic summary of the match, noting before the game started there had been an appeal for a certain doctor who had managed to get inside the packed stadium to return to a local hospital as soon as possible!

Donny Davies was also a great admirer of the Blackpool side who, of course, included Stanley Matthews on the right wing, but he also noted the classic inside forward play of Ernie Taylor who provided Matthews with a lot of telling passes. Ernie Taylor would two years later become a vital player for Manchester United in tragic circumstances...

Having gone a goal down in the first half, Donny Davies described the way both United's goals were created by Johnny Berry, but first the memorable sentence

"From the 10th minute until the interval, Blackpool were to suffer the tortures of a chicken having its neck rung by someone that had a mighty grip but was not quite competent enough to finish the job off quickly" He then explained Johnny Berry's importance, *"Who will forget Berry's serpentine dribble, when five defenders were left standing like lamp posts; or his final centre butted into by Doherty's head past goalkeeper Farm only to be butted out again by Firth standing on the goal line? Farm did not have one of his better days and whether or not he brought down Doherty who seemed to have lost possession, Johnny Berry certainly left him no chance of saving the resultant penalty. Farm and Berry were involved in United's winner as the goalkeeper could not hold Berry's short centre with the ball spilling to Tommy Taylor who hit the ball home"*

The final say on the day as the final whistle went was Donny Davies's information of the appeal given by Manchester United secretary Walter Crickmer over the loudspeaker,

"No presentation today chaps, if you please, go out in the normal exits so don't swarm over the pitch, thank you very much"

All neat and proper as people listened and acted on instructions in those days, still only eleven years after the war had ended.

The improvement they had shown over the 1955-56 season and the decisive manner of their eventual victory meant that United fans went into the 1956-57 season full of optimism. This time the team were determined to fight on three fronts. To defend their league title, to win the FA Cup and to conquer Europe. As champions, Manchester United would be representing England in the new European Cup competition, although the footballing authorities were firmly against their entry. Matt Busby and his board however were equally firm that they would compete. To get used to foreign opposition the club had again toured Scandinavia pre-season as Alf Clarke reported:

'As with last season, four matches were played and four victories achieved. In one of the matches against Helsingborg, Jackie Blanchflower actually played the match in goal as Ray Wood had to return to England, showing his versatility as he also played wing half, centre half and inside forward for the team'

The European story is covered in the next chapter. For the moment, we will concentrate on United's attempt to become the first team to win the double in the 20th century. United started the 1956-57 League campaign in the manner that they finished the previous game. After 12 games their record was W 10 D2 and also included a 1-0 defeat of Manchester City in the Charity Shield. There was now an air of inevitability of their League campaign.

The theme of floodlights has appeared throughout these extracts from the 'United Review' and when Portsmouth came to Old Trafford Tom Jackson spoke of some exciting developments for Old Trafford:

'With the involvement of European football and the continuing success of the club, Manchester United are about to finally get those floodlights the Old Trafford stadium needs, and deserves. Four 160 foot pylons would be each fitted with 54 floodlights. This will be too late for the start of the European Cup, but hopefully will be ready before the end of the season.'

The match itself only served to emphasise United's dominance of the league. Once more Donny Davies got to the heart of the matter in his report of a 3-0 victory over Portsmouth on the 3rd September 1956.

Association Football
CHAMPIONS ON TOP AGAIN
Portsmouth Fade After Bright Start
BY AN OLD INTERNATIONAL

Figure 44 Manchester Guardian, September 3, 1956

'No vaunting hyperbole is necessary to cry aloud the merits of Manchester United. Plain fact, modestly recorded will do as well. On Saturday at Old Trafford, United brushed aside Portsmouth's spirited challenge and beat them 3-0. Had the effort been necessary, it seemed well within the winner's powers to double the score.'

Others were less reserved. In a 3-part article in the Daily Mirror, running from 18th-20th-October 1956, Archie Ledbrooke and Frank McGhee pondered the *'Secrets of Success'* of *The greatest team in the world'*. If there was any doubt about their view on this United side the article started with this unequivocal opening:

'MANCHESTER UNITED are the greatest team and the greatest club in the world. THEY are the reigning champions of English soccer. THEY are a model for every other club in the league. THEY are unbeaten in 26 successive league games. Their supporters have forgotten what defeat tastes like.'

More was to follow:

They stroll out like young lions to toy with the opposition before chewing them up..........What heights (the team) will reach no-one can forecast. Busby is making no extravagant forecasts but it is clear that he thinks a league and cup double is possible. He thinks there is just one club in the country that has the skill, the talent, the fighting spirit

Figure 45 Daily Mirror, October 19. 1956

Figure 46 Daily Mirror, October 19, 1956

United's Victory
–Off The Pegg
MANCHESTER UNITED 6, ARSENAL 2

Figure 47 News of the World, February 10, 1957

and the resources to do it. NO PRIZES FOR GUESSING WHICH.'

Over the next two days the article went on to describe the 'secrets' United employed to bring the best to the club and develop them into stars. It made clear the central roles of Jimmy Murphy ('star spotter') and Bert Whalley ('star maker) in this process. Describing it thus:

THEY BELIEVE these youngsters are important.

THEY BELIEVE in making them feel like, and act like, important people.

THEY BELIEVE this will make them play like important people.'

The good form carried on into the New Year in the league. Donny Davies describing a 6-1 home victory over Newcastle likened it to carving a chicken.

'Manchester United carved up Newcastle United in an Association football match at Old Trafford, Manchester, on Saturday, with all the assurance of a practised host carving up a chicken. The score ended up 6-1 in the champions favour. Even the habitual croakers were satisfied'

Frank Swift reported on a similar home victory, 6-2 over Arsenal on the 9th February 1957. This time it was David Pegg who *'flashed out an urgent message to the F.A. selectors at Old Trafford. Six times the Arsenal net bulged, and five times the scoring move started with the tantalising United left-winger.*

With the league title looking secure United's attention diverted towards the FA Cup and Europe. Frank Swift described their progress to the FA Cup Final after a 2-0 win over Birmingham City in the semis.

UNITED NEARER THAT TREMENDOUS TREBLE
A Late Saver For Villa: Quick-Fire Goals End Birmingham Cup Hopes
BIRMINGHAM 0, MANCHESTER UNITED 1
Figure 48 News of the World, March 23, 1957

MANCHESTER UNITED regarded Birmingham as their stiffest Cup hurdle – but the Busby Babes took the game in their stride to qualify for Wembley with relative ease. Off to the tonic of two goals in the first quarter of an hour, United's speedy young footballers dominated the game from then on. Manchester United fans needn't have worried about the absence of centre-forward Tommy Taylor. Dennis Viollet switched to lead the attack, gave City centre-half, Trevor Smith, a punishing afternoon. And for young Bobby

Charlton, who came on at inside-left, it marked a dream Cup debut. This nephew of Cup-fighter Jackie Milburn nobly carried on the family tradition – first by giving Johnny Berry the pass that led to the opening goal, and then by scoring with his first shot in a Cup-tie.

By ARCHIE LEDBROOKE

Figure 49 Daily Mirror, March 26, 1957

Finally, the new Old Trafford floodlights were ready for display in all their glory for the visit of Bolton Wanderers in late March 1957. Both Alf Clarke and Tom Jackson had plenty of information for the fans. Alf Clarke felt they looked like the Yankee Stadium in New York and wondered if international matches would be played at Old Trafford. He also noted that the United kit of that night, all red, would bring the following comment, *'They will be calling Manchester United The Red Devils next.'* Stealing the name of the local Salford Rugby League side who were known as The Red Devils. Tom Jackson confirmed that Real Madrid would be the opponents in the European Cup semi-final and that it would be the first ever European Cup tie to be held at Old Trafford. The match itself proved an anti-climax as United went down 2-0 to bogey side Bolton Wanderers in what Archie Ledbrooke described as a *'Disaster by Floodlight'*.

FANS RUSH IN—TOO SOON

Figure 50 Daily Mirror, April 30, 1957

Despite the blip, the league was won again, this time by 8 points. Reporting on the last league game of the season Archie Ledbrooke described the scene as fans rushed on the pitch prematurely having mistaken the referee's whistle for full-time. After the match, Captain Roger Byrne had the following message to the fans:

'If you give us the support we have had during the past two seasons, there is no reason why we shouldn't pull off a hat trick of League championships next year.'

With one trophy in the bag, it was with a mood of optimism that United prepared for the FA Cup Final and the first double of the century. Despite this, some felt that United's efforts on three fronts would take their toll on the team. Frank Swift dismissed the notion in no uncertain terms.

United Stale? Not Likely

By FRANK SWIFT

"*MANCHESTER UNITED have burned themselves out; Villa for the Cup." I quote just one example of the hysterical chatter that has buzzed the rounds since the European Cup exit of England's League champions.*

Figure 51 News of the World, April 28, 1957

Writing about the *'hysterical chatter'*, Swift dismissed this out of hand. He went on to make an insightful point about the experience the team had gained in Europe:

'The European Cup has conditioned United

to the big occasions. There will be no fear of Cup Final nerves.'

The next chapter describes United's European Cup journey. Swift's quote though supports Matt Busby's intention that European competition would further the team's education. For now, onto the F.A. Cup Final.

And so, Manchester United went to Wembley Stadium for the FA Cup Final against Aston Villa full of confidence. Roy Cavanagh had the honour of interviewing Matt Busby for

ASTON VILLA'S RECORD OF CUP VICTORIES

Handicapped champions fight to the last

BY AN OLD INTERNATIONAL

Figure 52 Manchester Guardian, May 6, 1957

another book he was involved in and he told him that on the morning of the match he was up early and went to visit all the players. If they were well there was no way they could lose the match he felt. They were all well, at least until the sixth minute........

Nine years after reporting on the 1948 Final Donny Davies was back at Wembley to see United foiled in their attempt to record what would have been the first League and FA Cup Double in the 20th Century. Unlike 1948, this time he was to be disappointed. Characteristically though, he kept his poise. Magnanimously describing the unfolding drama that saw United down to 10 men after just 6 minutes as keeper Ray Wood's suffered a fractured cheek bone:

'Tragedy was again lurking offstage. Waiting only for the sixth minute to rob United of the services of their regular goalkeeper for most of the match, and rob Villa too of much of the credit for their narrow 2-1 victory.'

While declining to criticise Villa forward Peter McParland directly, for what, even by the standards of the time, was verging on assault, Donny Davies wondered why England was the only remaining FA to allow the goalkeeper to be charged, stating that there was....

'....a growing body of opinion that England should follow the lead of the rest of the world and adopt their rule that as soon as the goalkeeper has the ball in his hands he should be immune from all forms of manhandling. Any more brash interpretations of the charging rule, like Saturday's, and we shall have the "goalkeeper's friendly society" demanding that in future goalkeepers should be able to enter the field in crash helmets and wearing padded garments like American footballers. Heaven protects us from this spectacle.'

Jackie Blanchflower donned the goalkeeper's jersey. Remarkably, Ray Woods bravely returned to the field but as a makeweight right-wing for all but the last seven minutes when he went back in goal as United fought desperately to equalise after Taylor clawed back a goal to reduce the deficit to 2-1. Whelan had the ball in the net, but it was ruled offside and eventually despite fighting to the last United's dream was ended.

Matt Busby did not blunder

By ERIC THOMPSON

Figure 53 Daily Mail, May 6, 1957

Some considered that Busby should have asked Wood to go back in goal earlier, but Eric Thompson, interviewed Wood after the game and begged to differ.

'At the after-the-match banquet Wood told me: "I kept feeling stabs of pain. If I had gone into goal earlier I should probably have fallen down between the posts." Busby said "He should never have come out at all in the second half. I was surprised to see him trot out into the arena. During the interval we tried him with a ball at the back of the stadium, but he wasn't seeing it properly.'

The last word on the matter should perhaps go to retired goalkeeper Frank Swift. While acknowledging that United's double bid had effectively ended in the sixth minute Swift was quick to praise the heroics of stand in goalkeeper Jackie Blanchflower.

'Centre-half Jackie Blanchflower was a magnificent deputy in the Manchester goal....... Not that Wood would have had any chance with the goals that beat Blanchflower. The inspired Irishman was the main reason that Villa did not take the champions to the cleaners properly.'

CHAPTER FIVE
THE JOURNEY INTO EUROPE

In 2016 Britain voted to leave the European Union of 28 nations, a policy which would become known as Brexit. Sixty years earlier, Manchester United, via the leadership of their manager Matt Busby, decided to go in the other direction. United ignored the wishes (orders really!) of the Football League by accepting an entry into the second season of the European Cup. The European Cup was then a competition solely for champions, which in 1956/57 was comprised of 22 clubs, the 21 champions of the competing nations and Real Madrid the previous seasons winners. This, therefore, gave Spain two teams as their champions were actually Athletic Bilbao.

Matt Busby strongly felt that his side, which already were being dubbed 'The Busby Babes' now needed further football education by experiencing the foreign way of playing. Three years earlier, in November 1953, Hungary had visited Wembley Stadium to play England and shattered their unbeaten home record against foreign opposition by winning 6-3, and winning easily. The following May, Hungary fully emphasised this result by beating England 7-1 in Budapest. England could not ignore this marvellous football, and certainly Matt Busby did not ignore it. He emphasised to his board that Manchester United must enter, and challenge this different type of football. He was fully aware of the League's opposition, even though he could not accept it, and felt that Chelsea had let English football down the previous season when they acceded to the League's dictate not to enter. It would create a simmering tension between the Football League and Manchester United, so much so that the former would take every chance to hammer home to United their perceived mistake if they could.

Figure 54 Match Tickets 1956-57 European Campaign

Matt Busby had been appointed manager of Manchester United on October 22, 1945 and the size of the task facing him and Manchester United was huge. They had already had to overcome the fact that when football returned from the 1946/47 season they would not have a home ground to call their own as Old Trafford had been badly blitzed in the early years of the Second World War, and they had not to just reconstruct the ground but had the added problem of players resuming their careers after the deprivation of war.

The team, though, was suffering for those six years of lost war time action and disruption to life and were becoming an aged side. Matt Busby and his trusted right hand man, Jimmy Murphy, had turned to a youth policy and by the early 1950's signs were that young footballers from all corners of the British Isles were arriving at Old Trafford. So, the arrival of this foreign competition pitting his young players with the players from across Europe was a real impetus to see how far they had come, and could go.

CUP WIN FOR THE CHAMPS

MANCHESTER United, Football League champions, beat the Belgian club Anderlecht 2—0 at Brussels last night in the first leg of their first round European Cup match.

Dennis Viollet scored the first goal in the twenty-third minute; Tommy Taylor got the other, fifteen minutes before the end.

Figure 55 Daily Mirror, September 13, 1956

In those early days of the European Cup competition, the drawn clubs decided the dates of their matches between themselves, and it would be a visit to Brussels to meet the mighty Belgian Champions, RSC Anderlecht in September 1956 that Manchester United played their first ever European tie.

A reflection of the negative view of the competition, can be seen in the tiny match report that was included in the following morning's Daily Mirror. The report featured alongside much more extensive reports of Gillingham v Swindon and Hull v Workington. As is so often the case Manchester led the way though, and the two Manchester papers were much more positive. The Manchester Guardian carried a full report, which in amongst the usual brilliantly crafted details of the match by Donny Davies, included these fascinating details. The team was a source of immense pride, the war battered stadiums back home were not…..

'If one wants to feel British and proud of it, travel around with Manchester United. The reverence with which their players are received in Belgium stems from the detailed knowledge of the clubs achievements…'

'Its (The Emile Versé Stadium) *grandstands or tribunes as they are called, with their cantilever roofs and no obstructing pillars are a reproach to many clumsy old-fashioned erections at home. It offered a scene of unforgettable beauty as the game started with the pitch flooded in cool silvery light, giving it a sense of theatre'*

Indeed although a 2-0 victory was a marvellous start, the second leg would have to be played across Manchester at City's home ground of Maine Road as Old Trafford would not have their floodlights until March 1957.

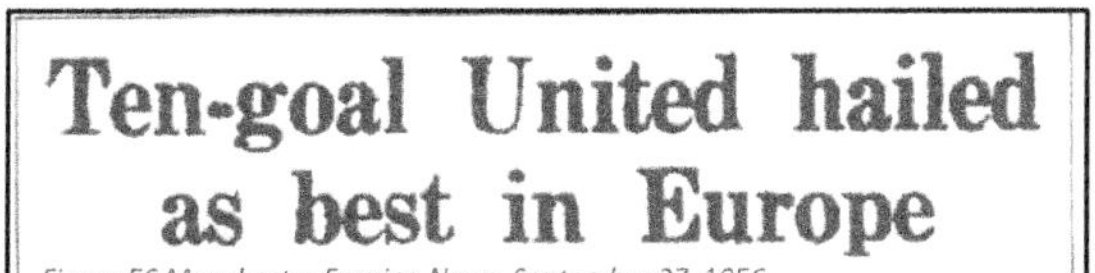

Ten-goal United hailed as best in Europe

Figure 56 Manchester Evening News, September 27, 1956

An interesting illustration of the importance of the press is provided by Roy Cavanagh's recollections from the time: *'Even though United had that two goal advantage, I can still remember clearly as a ten year old looking at one of the Manchester Evening papers of the time as they reviewed that night's return match. The paper showed pictures of the Anderlecht players along with brief bios of the players. It made them sound like supermen. When I woke up the following morning it was to learn the Manchester United had won 10-0 on the night and 12-0 on aggregate!'*

While the national press were still seemingly reluctant to report on the game the performance couldn't fail to grab people's attention. There was no doubt that United would be provided with a stern challenge to be the very best in Europe. Even so many believed it was a challenge they were more than capable of meeting. Tom Jackson in the Manchester Evening News interviewed Anderlecht's captain, Jeff Mermans after the game. In the interview he stated: *'There is not a single excuse we can offer for our humiliating defeat. We gave our best, but it was just not good enough against what must rate as one of the best club teams in the world.'*

Figure 57 Daily Express, October 18, 1956

Next came Borussia Dortmund. The national newspapers still continued their scant reporting of United's European Cup adventures. Henry Rose's report in the Daily Express was smaller than a report on a friendly between Headington United (now Oxford United) and an All Star XI and much smaller than coverage of England's U23's 0-0 draw with France on the same night. The crowd increase of nearly 30,000 to a full house of 75,000 testified to the enthusiasm of the fans though. Incidentally, this was then the highest crowd for a floodlight match in England.

The fans though had a demand that the ten goal rout of Anderlecht in the previous tie would be equalled at least against the German champions, and when Manchester United swept into a 3-0 lead, via two Dennis Viollet goals and an own goal, their demands seemed justified. Henry Rose joined their thoughts as he said, *'Three goals by United before half time against a side of part timers with an average age of 30 surely had settled the tie in the first half.'* By the end though, as Dortmund scored two unanswered goals, Henry Rose had real concerns as he said, *'Manchester United, wonder team of the Football League are human after all. Instead of the cricket score so many expected of them against the Germans at Maine Road they just scraped through leaving their hopes on the line for the second leg.'*

Backed by thousands of British troops based in West Germany, Manchester United produced one of their finest back to the wall defensive displays over in Dortmund for the second leg. With Duncan Edwards deployed in the forward line for the injured Dennis Viollet in this match, it was a brilliant team display with goalkeeper Ray Wood and full back and captain Roger Byrne turning in their finest United performances, and on a very tricky pitch as Archie Ledbrooke recalled. *'On the frosted ground, which made the ball bounce crazily and the players lose their footing, United had to survive a blitzing as they held out for a 0-0 draw to go through to the next round.'*

George Follows report followed suit really, praising the back to the wall defensive display that Messrs Wood, Foulkes, Byrne, Jones and young Wilf McGuinness, playing at number six as Duncan was in the forward line, put in. *The red shirts of Manchester United put in an heroic rear-guard display to hold a mighty German soccer blitz here tonight.'*

Airlift For These Globe-trotting Fans

Figure 58 News of the World, January 13, 1957

United's success had begun to capture the public imagination. So much so that a small, but growing, army of fans had begun to follow the team abroad. Frank Swift interviewed one of the fans about to fly to the next tie in Bilbao for a two night stay for the princely sum of £29.

The continental engagements of the league champions have given their supporters a chance to prove that they will follow the Busby Babes to the end of the earth – if they can afford it. "Cheap at the price" is the verdict of one of them. Sam Smith, a keen United fan that runs the Swan Hotel, Crumpsall. Many of Sam's companions were cheering United

Figure 59 Daily Mirror, January 17, 1957

on with him in Dortmund, where they even had a police motorcycle escort to the ground. On the flight back they told the air-charter firm **"Put our names down for the next round"** *- before they knew what opposition was in store for them in the next round.' Now they are looking forward to a football fiesta on Jan 16th - and you can bet your life that Sam and Co. will be queuing for the next Air-Special if they get through to the semi-finals.'*

Who said Sunny Spain?! When the Manchester United party arrived in Northern Spain in mid-January 1957, it certainly was not sunny, indeed it was a mixture of snow, sleet and rain as the packed crowd all seemed to have umbrellas up! The Basque region is a very passionate, partisan part of Spain and that was reflected by the noise made by the crowd, despite the atrocious conditions. Bilbao were actually the champions of Spain but as Real Madrid had won the previous season's final, Spain had two sides in the competition. It soon became apparent how good Bilbao were though as they scythed through the mud, helped by a couple of United mistakes, to go 3-0 up at half time. United did recover and pulled two goals back through Tommy Taylor and Dennis Viollet, but when Bilbao restored their three goal advantage at 5-2 and roars of support boomed out it looked as though Manchester United's European Cup dream would be coming to an end. Then the unassuming inside right Billy Whelan produced a quite magnificent goal out of nothing as he seemed to waltz through the mud and the Bilbao defence to score a vital third goal for United. This ray of hope was seized on by reporters Archie Ledbrooke and Henry Rose.

Archie's report now merited a full page article in the Daily Mirror as he described what he had seen,' *A snowstorm raged throughout on a treacherous black and white swamp---in which Bilbao's centre half Garay was United's abominable snowman.*' Henry Rose also filed a full report in typical forthright fashion. Rose had no doubt that United would overturn the two-goal deficit on home turf. *'British hearts are high here tonight, and the man who is responsible for that is a broth of a boy from Dublin, 21 year old Bill Whelan. Oh yes, Bilbao won 5-3 but after seeing this eight goal thriller I'm quite sure the League Champions will scrub out the two goal margin in the second leg at Manchester on 6th February and go into the semi-final of the European Cup.'*

The Manchester Evening News brought a bit of humour by showing a cartoon of leading reporter Tom Jackson in a sombrero on the phone sending his match report.

Figure 60 Daily Mirror,
January 18, 1957

Before Manchester United could even think about overturning a two goal deficit, they had to get home from 'Sunny Spain'! On reaching the Bilbao airfield, the plane was snowbound and the airport closed. The penalty to United for failing to return for the forthcoming Saturday fixture at Sheffield Wednesday would be severe as the footballing authorities were still fuming that United had gone against their wishes and entered the European Cup in the first place. Any opportunity to put them back in their place would be manna from heaven for them.

Archie Ledbrooke recalled the sight that met the player's eyes and the incredible events that followed.

The players physically manhandled the aircraft across the runway. They searched for brushes, broom heads, anything which would be able to work on the ice and snow. They started on the tail, across the fuselage across the wings. When there was a sign they could perhaps fly the players and journalists all had to load their own luggage. Incredibly, remember the airport was closed, the plane took off in a blizzard with minimal visibility. It landed in Jersey for a refuel in glorious sunshine and reached Manchester three hours later than scheduled.'

A measure of the interest that United's European journey was creating is provided by the front page of the Manchester Evening News on the day of the return leg. The whole of the front page was dedicated to the match. The danger men of the 'Bounding Basques' were pictured and described in detail – in Spanish too. As well as Tom Jackson's view of the match there is an interesting contribution from Willie Lomas – claiming that the United side he recalled from 1909 would have been a match for the Busby Babes!

Figure 61 Manchester Evening News, February 6, 1957

Figure 62 Daily Mirror, February 11, 1957

Unbeknown to the fans at that time was while preparing for the second leg Bilbao actually tried to prise Matt Busby away from the club he was building to a much better paid life in Spain. Reporting after the match Archie Ledbrooke reported that Bilbao offered Busby the 'princely' sum of £5,000 per year to manage their team. Fortunately for United, Busby turned the offer down 'emphatically'.

Figure 63 Manchester Evening News, February 7, 1957

There was immediate justification for Busby's decision. The 3-0 victory which overturned the tie 6-5 in Manchester United's favour, is often recalled as one of Manchester United's greatest ever victories. Dennis Viollet, with his ninth goal of the tournament so far, Tommy Taylor and a late Johnny Berry tie clincher sealed an incredible night of football by Manchester United. Henry Rose even described it as the *'Greatest victory in soccer history'*. George Follows described it as, *'the greatest football match he had ever seen, the greatest crowd he had ever heard, and the greatest centre forward display by Tommy Taylor he had ever known'*

Whilst as usual, Donny Davies was not lost for words either, he even finished by quoting Rupert Brook's poem 'The Dead';

Taylor changed feet, foxing the great Garay and scored the goal of his career. This time the crowd's roar of exultation was deafening and still fifteen minutes was left to play. When Berry had scored the third decisive goal and the final whistle went, there are no words to describe the closing moments. Never has Manchester greater reason to be proud of her representatives.

"Honour had come back as a king to earth
And paid his subjects with a royal wage'"

Figure 64 Daily Mirror, February 8, 1957

A footnote to the matches against Dortmund & Bilbao is provided by what was a growing issue around player bonuses. Archie Ledbrooke reported in the Mirror that United had requested permission from the Football League to pay their players 'international' win bonuses of £50. This was still way off what their opponents were paying. Reporting from Bilbao Tom Jackson claimed that in comparison the Spaniards were on, what must have been an eye watering, £200 per man win bonus. Roger Byrne voiced the player's frustrations to Archie Ledbrooke.

'We know that the Dortmund players were on a £100 TV set each to beat us. We know that Bilbao were on something like £200 a man to lick us. We have read that Real Madrid were on something like £400 a man in last year's final. So we have drawn up a list of the bonuses we suggest.'

The League refused and so United had to stick to the maximum £3 win bonus plus £3 match fee!

It was to be a return to Spain for the semi-final, and this time the weather was the expected warmth of a spring like Madrid. Matt Busby had actually gone over to Nice to see the second leg of the Nice v Real Madrid quarter final tie, accompanied by some of the English press corps who were now enthralled by the performances of the Manchester United team and wanted to bring to the public knowledge of their next opponents. Matt Busby knew, however, as he saw Madrid ease through to meet his young side that the hardest possible assignment awaited his team…

No-penalty referee is cheered by Madrid

Real Madrid .... 3 Manchester United 1

Figure 65 Daily Mail, April 12, 1957

Real Madrid had won the inaugural competition the season before and they possessed a very worldly side which just oozed experience and, at times, cynical know how to complement their exquisite skill. One player in particular, had been quickly identified by Matt Busby in Nice as being the ring master of the Madrid side, centre forward Alfredo Di Stefano.

In the end the first leg tie was a special event which still lives in the club's history, even though the end result was 3-1 to Real Madrid. Before the match, the atmosphere in Madrid was electric. Everybody wanted to see and meet the famous Manchester United who had done the impossible and knocked out Bilbao after giving them a two goal start. Frank Taylor told of an interesting telephone call to the hotel reception. *'Ah, Mr Taylor, you are the famous Tommy Taylor of Manchester United. This is one of the flamenco dancers from Mr Antonio's troupe who entertained your club. Is it possible to get a ticket for the game tomorrow? I had to break in, 'Madam, I am NOT Tommy Taylor, and quickly passed the phone over to Tommy!'*

When the game started, United had competed strongly in the first half which ended goalless, so much so that Madrid used some very strong arm stuff to unsettle their young opponents. George Follows particularly was annoyed at the antics of Di Stefano, who despite being a magnificent footballer, was also a very worldly one. George noted,

'Real Madrid got away with murder in front of a crowd estimated as many as 130,000 at the Santiago Bernebau Stadium today who had paid a world record £55,000 in receipts. They hacked, slashed, kicked and wrestled their way, with a kick by Di Stefano on Jackie Blanchflower being particularly vicious. Marquitos, the centre half was the worst culprit though, and the Dutch referee Leo Horn was far too lenient with the Madrid players. There really seemed no need for the Spaniards to use such foul and intimidating methods, however,

their attitude was a mark of respect for just how much they feared United'

Even so, there was no doubting the class of the Real Madrid side. Eric Thompson described their key players in concise, accurate terms:

'This Madrid forward line is full of world-class players. Di Stefano, strolling through the game with a master's confidence, could not be curbed by Colman. Gento had a razor-edge of speed that worried Foulkes and Kopa kept flashing into sparkling solos.'

Thompson remained confident the Babes could pull things back in the return leg, in a game where there would be *'More of an English atmosphere, less of the Continental excitability about the game'.*

Figure 66 News of the World, April 14, 1957

Frank Swift was more pessimistic though: *'This is the story I didn't want to write. It is one I never expected to write when I sat with 120,000 fans in the fabulous Santiago de Bernabeau Stadium, waiting to see how the pride of Europe, Madrid would fare against Britain's best soccer side, Manchester United, in the first leg of the European Cup semi-finals. But it must be said that the sheer brilliance of the Spanish team will smash the hopes of a soccer treble when they visit Old Trafford for the return match on Thursday week.*

Figure 67 Daily Mail, April 25, 1957

Having their new floodlights opened a few weeks earlier, what a mouth-watering prospect to see the European champions. Everybody it seemed wanted to see the Spanish masters, with such famous sporting stars of the area such as Cyril Washbrook the Lancashire and England cricketer, and the great Tommy Finney the Preston North End and England footballer amongst the full house. Manchester United wore a special all red kit for the occasion and Madrid, in their famous all white strip looked magical against the green Old Trafford pitch. Mind you, whilst it was supposed to be all green, Matt Busby had insisted that lots of water be sprayed on the pitch, hoping to stem the quick ball playing skills of the multinational Real Madrid side. In the end, the skills of the reigning champions proved too much as they scored twice in the first half to take an unassailable 5-1 aggregate into the second half. Manchester United however, repaid all Matt Busby's faith by coming out and showing there immense promise as the equalised at 2-2 on the night but had to go out of the competition on a 5-3 aggregate.

Interestingly the home leg reports in the Express and Mirror were by Desmond Hackett & Frank McGhee in place of their Northern

Correspondents Henry Rose and Archie Ledbrooke. Was this a reflection of the growing national interest in the Busby Babes' journey? As ever, Donny Davies was there to pen another of his mini masterpieces. While the Mirror & Express focus on the lack of sportsmanship and booing from the crowd, he had a more positive viewpoint:

'Real Madrid made themselves the toast of two hemispheres and Manchester United the toast of all English speaking peoples when they drew 2-2 at Old Trafford tonight in the semi-finals of the European Cup...... Bedlam after this will hold no terrors. One had thought that the notion that great deeds could be wrought by a vast concentration of noise had died with Joshua. But the Manchester dailies and the Manchester crowd had other ideas and if noise could have served their purpose they would have won hands down.'

Figure 69 Daily Mail, April 26, 1957

Eric Thompson in the Daily Mail also commented on the boos: *'Boos, backslaps and more boos. What a finish to the headline-hogging European Cup semi-final at Old Trafford last night, with the holders Real Madrid leaping into the centre of the floodlit arena to give their farewell whoops and bows, and the crowd responding with the biggest boo of a boo-oo night. The crowd overdid the booing. But Madrid did give them a lot of cause with their body checks.'*

Figure 68 Match Ticket 1957-58 European Campaign

Manchester United comfortably retained their League championship to provide themselves with another crack at the European Cup for the 1957/8 season. This time the Football League did not object (at least outwardly) and Matt Busby knew his side would be extremely well prepared and equipped to take on Europe's finest, including Real Madrid if they were to meet again. Madrid, incidentally, retained their trophy after knocking United out in the semi-final by beating Italian champions Fiorentina in the Final.

Figure 70 Manchester Evening News, September 26, 1957

Having got used to travelling to some of Europe's major cities, it was a short hop over the Irish Sea to meet the Irish champions Shamrock Rovers at the start of the 1957/8 campaign. Dublin was in the grasp of a wild windy night, so much so that the referee and the two sides decided they would only have a five minute half time break and so made a quick turn round! A crushing 6-0 victory for United in a city already with many supporters of United, effectively closed the tie off at the first go. Tom Jackson, was hungry for more though, speculating that the eventual margin might exceeded the 12-0 aggregate margin over Anderlecht in last season's competition.

SHAMROCK ROVERS PUT UP A MAGNIFICENT FIGHT
Manchester United win by one goal
BY AN OLD INTERNATIONAL

Figure 71 Manchester Guardian, October 3, 1957

In fact, Shamrock Rovers produced a very spirited response in the second leg at Old Trafford before going down 3-2. This earned United a first trip behind the 'Iron Curtain' to play a competitive match, a visit to Prague to meet the famous Czechoslovakian champions Dukla. The home tie was played first. This match was actually played a week after the intended date, indeed the match programme shows the original date. This was due to the sudden death of the Czechoslovakian National President and so the team, which was full of Czechoslovakian army personnel, had to return to Prague. After a goalless first half, Eric Thompson in the 'Daily Mail' described a second half transformation,

Three second half goals should be enough for Manchester United, who can expect to move forward in the European Cup for a second year. Dukla had played excellently defensively in the first half, but do not seem to have enough power to trouble United in Prague. Even though United had to find a replacement for the injured Dennis Viollet, they did just that and Wales international Colin Webster was the scorer of two of United's three second half unanswered goals.'

Holding a comfortable 3-0 lead from the first leg, Manchester United were quietly confident as they made their first trip behind the 'Iron Curtain' to play in the Czechoslovakian capital of Prague. Eric Thompson made the journey, and in his report on the day before the match he described the frozen conditions of the snow covered pitch, making the choice of boots difficult for the United players. There was heavy rain at the time of the match, with Manchester United's trip to the National Army Stadium being up winding streets to the ground which was on top of a hill overlooking Prague. Dukla took a first half lead but United held out, although as Archie Ledbrooke reported, they were robbed of an equaliser:

'Tommy Taylor scored what seemed a perfectly good equaliser in the seventy second minute, until the Dukla players protested that Taylor had been offside and the German referee eventually agreed with them. Eddie Colman certainly did not deserve to be on the losing side, it was the poor performance of their attack that cost them the tie on the night but not on aggregate.'

The tensions between Manchester United and the Football League over the club actually playing in the European Cup surfaced again after the second leg tie in Prague. United had to get a ferry back to England as part of a 1,000 mile journey. With England being fog bound there was real concerns that the team would not get back in time to fulfil their away fixture against Birmingham City on the Saturday. Fog was also enveloping Amsterdam airport where the team were to make a stop and so their plane was diverted to Frankfurt. In the end, the journalists had to stay to get another plane home whilst the players made a ferry trip to Harwich en route for their Birmingham fixture. A further problem was finding facilities to treat three injured players to give them a chance of playing on the Saturday. Matt Busby was acutely aware that if they had not managed to play the Birmingham match the Football League would come down hard on the club, probably banning them from continuing their European campaign.

Manchester United had not so far that season had an exclusive charter flight for their European adventures, after the vicissitudes of the journey from Prague, the club decided this was the last time they would leave travel to chance and decided from the next tie that they would actually hire their own charter flight to wherever they were sent. It would be again behind the 'Iron Curtain', this time to the Yugoslavian capital of Belgrade to play their champions, Red Star…

Why the two clubs decided on a mid-January Old Trafford first leg and an early February date for a Belgrade visit for the second leg is surprising as, in the event, the semi-final would not take place until May. When that first leg arrived, Manchester United were in prime position for an unprecedented treble, as they were nicely placed in the top three in the League, although leaders Wolverhampton Wanderers were having a fine season, they were through to the 4th round of the FA Cup (a game they would win 2-0 against Ipswich Town) and, of course, now in the quarter finals of the European Cup for a second successive season.

Manchester United had gone through a difficult period after the Dukla Prague ties and Matt Busby had made quite radical changes for his way of managership. A world record fee for a goalkeeper £23,000, had been paid for Northern Ireland International Harry Gregg who was playing at the then Second Division Doncaster Rovers. Three of the well-known United 'Busby Babes' line up, wingers Johnny Berry and David Pegg, along with free scoring inside forward Bill Whelan were all dropped to bring in Ken Morgans, Albert Scanlon and Bobby Charlton. The changes made an immediate impact and United were on an eight match unbeaten run when the champions of Yugoslavia, Red Star Belgrade arrived at Old Trafford in mid January 1958.

The home programme against Red Star Belgrade had both Alf Clarke and Tom Jackson giving their comments. Alf gave a view of a 'Festival of Britain' match in 1951 whilst Tom give a detailed report on the, relatively, short history of Red Star who had only been formed after the war. The Manchester fog, rolling in off the Ship Canal, made matters difficult in the first leg. Archie Ledbrooke wrote *'Red Star showed they had not made the trip without fancying their chances.'* Indeed, they took a first half lead, with Ledbrooke describing how:

'Suddenly Red Star had begun to sparkle. For the next ten minutes United found it difficult to hold out against the accurate short passing of the Yugoslav team. Then they cracked.'

Manchester United responded with goals from young players Bobby Charlton and a rare Eddie Colman goal giving United a slight 2-1 advantage to take to Belgrade for the second leg. Eric Thompson brilliantly captures the fighting spirit of the Babes that saw them emerge 2-1 winners. A lead that Thompson considered would be enough.

'The margin may just be enough to see them through, but it is perilously slender against a team like Red Star. United did not snatch victory in this pulsating match because of any notable improvement on their disappointing first-half play, but because they seemed to chase and press and tackle like men with glowing coals in their boots.'

RED DEVILS SHOW THAT OLD FIGHT
By GEORGE FOLLOWS
Manchester United 2, Red Star (Belgrade) 1

Figure 73 Daily Herald - January 15, 1958

George Follows also headlined with a comment on the 'Red Devils' fighting spirit. He also reported on an interesting night for Harry Gregg making his European debut.

'Red Star had shown no sign of scoring a goal when in the 33rd minute, inside forward Tasic picked the ball up thirty yards from goal, looked up to see Gregg off his goal line and lobbed him to leave Manchester United's Irish goalkeeper embarrassed by his mistake. Now, it was a very foggy night at Old Trafford, but I think Harry will be the first to hold his hand up and admit his error. At least second half goals from Bobby Charlton and a very rare Eddie Colman winner, would see Harry off happier to play for Northern Ireland in their World Cup tie with Italy the following night.'

Yes, you have not misread that, Harry Gregg played a European Cup tie on the Tuesday night and was flying over to Belfast for a World Cup tie the following night although in the end he did not play due to a knock.

The second leg was to be played in Belgrade on Wednesday 5th February with an afternoon kick off due to their lack of floodlights. On the Saturday previous, Manchester United played Arsenal at Highbury in what turned out to be a game that would forever go into the club's folklore. A quite brilliant all round team performance saw United lead 3-0 at half time, only for Arsenal to send the full house of over 63,000 wild as they equalised at 3-3. United responded brilliantly to go back 5-3 in front before Arsenal pulled a late goal back, but not enough to stop Manchester United travelling back in great heart, a second leg European Cup tie in Belgrade and then a top of the League match against Wolverhampton Wanderers to play in the next seven days…

Figure 74 Players and journalists prepare to board at Ringway Airport

CHAPTER SIX
THE LAST MATCH, THE LAST REPORTS

A visit to Belgrade in early February would not be on most people's travel lists, certainly not in 1958, as only two years after the uprising against communism in neighbouring Hungary, had got many minds fixed on freedom and a better life after the terrible pain inflicted on countries all across Europe during the Second World War.

Remember that the war had only ended thirteen years earlier and rationing in Britain had only been lifted in 1954, so for the travelling party of players, journalists, BEA staff, Mr & Mrs Miklos who were the couple who had organised the Manchester United travel arrangements when playing in Europe, Mrs Lukic the wife of the Yugoslav attaché in London and her baby, and Willie Satinoff, a wealthy Manchester businessman, a racehorse owner, close friend of Matt Busby and probable next Manchester United director, what greeted them around Belgrade was austere to say the least. The city was under snow although intermittent sunshine was trying to break through and give some thaw, so they were immediate doubts as to the condition of the pitch at the stadium, which was actually the home of Partizan Belgrade and the Yugoslav International side as Red Star's ground was deemed inadequate for such a prestigious match.

Donny Davies reported in the Guardian on the morning of the match *'that Manchester United had two main preoccupations, the state of the National Stadium, and the injury captain and left back Roger Byrne had sustained at Highbury the previous Saturday against Arsenal. Trainer Tom Curry had worked very hard on Byrne's injury and he was expected to be fit. There was also good news about the pitch which the slight thaw had made the chances of playing virtually certain.'*

All 55,000 tickets had been sold for the game, despite the fact the stadium was virtually all open to the elements. The Yugoslavian public were very well informed about this young English side that had already taken Europe by storm over the past couple of seasons. Such was the interest in Yugoslavia that stories were flying around that Marshall Tito, the President of the country, may even attend the match. It was reported that two Americans visited the Metropol Hotel where United were staying looking for a couple of tickets and were prepared to pay fabulous amounts to get them, but they had no luck. It was also announced that if the tie had been all square at the end of the second leg (no away goals or penalties in those days) the third match was arranged to be played in Milan.

Dennis Viollet recalled the scenes that met some of the players as they visited the centre of Belgrade on the Tuesday. *"We were still suffering in Manchester from the aftermath of the war, and rationing had only just finished. But this place was bad, really bad. We felt so sorry for the people especially the older ones and the children. We were amazed to see people walking around without shoes, despite the bad weather, some had used old tyres as makeshift footwear. If this was what communism was like, then they could keep it".*

Come match day on the Wednesday and everyone was in high spirits as they knew they had to get the game sorted then fly back to Manchester the day after. The stadium was full, a lot of army personnel around either as supporters or to keep the piece. United only had a slender 2-1 lead but the volume of noise was burst within the first twenty minutes as goals from Dennis Violet and young Bobby Charlton put United in total command of the match and the tie. This was sealed (or so it seemed) when Charlton scored his second and United's third to take into a half time 3-0 score line, 5-1 on aggregate. There had been a couple of worries, Kenny Morgans had received a very bad injury with his thigh ripped open by a bad tackle whilst Duncan Edwards was also concerned about an ankle injury, although actually nothing seemed to concern Big Duncan!.

Red Star Belgrade did, however, have a genuine world class inside forward called Dragoslav Sekularac, a very talented footballer who was then only twenty years old but would become a world famous footballer. He orchestrated Red Star's comeback, although it has to be said, with the generous help of the Austrian referee who gave some strange decisions against United which resulted in goals from a dubious penalty and a free kick given the wrong way on the edge of United's penalty area which resulted in an equaliser at 3-3 on the day, but Manchester United still having that vital 5-4 aggregate in their favour. When the final whistle went the United players quickly got back to their dressing room where bottles of beer were welcome relief after the last forty five minutes. The team was euphoric, they had reached a second consecutive European Cup semi-final and they knew they were now really well equipped for whatever European sides had to throw at them.

Captain Roger Byrne informed the press, *'I have never wanted to hear the final whistle more than I did today. Red Star were much better than in Manchester, particularly in the second half. Now we are in the semi-finals I hope we get Real Madrid again as this year I feel we can run them much closer.'*

As had become customary after European matches there was the official banquets to attend in the British Embassy before groups of the players and journalists broke off in common friendship, either back to the team's hotel or to see what Belgrade had to offer at night. This bond was very strong with really good, trustworthy friendships made as 'what happened abroad stayed what happened abroad'. Such as Dennis Viollet, Bobby Charlton and Frank Swift the News of the World journalist, but also of course, the former Manchester City and England great goalkeeper, went off with some Embassy staff although Big Swifty felt a stomach issue coming on so returned to the hotel, whilst others found some club to visit and others played cards until late back at the team's hotel. As they say, 'Tomorrow is another day' but for far too many it would be their last day.

Figure 75 Ticket & Match Programme from Belgrade

With the exception of Frank Swift who wrote for The News of The World (published on Sunday), the journalists at the match had already filed their reports for the Thursday morning editions, here is what they said:

ALF CLARKE

The referee nearly scared United out of European Cup

Figure 76 Manchester Evening Chronicle, February 6, 1958

Manchester United were almost frightened out of the European Cup - by the referee. I have played and watched football for more than forty years, but I have never seen a referee make so many appalling decisions as Herr Kainer. Whatever rules the referee used they were certainly not those used by FIFA or UEFA. To me they were something he had made up himself.

Too Scared

I do not wish to detract from Red Stars' brilliant second-half football – but with the referee accompanying every United tackle with a whistle the United players eventually became scared to challenge for the football.

It seems almost impossible for any team to give United a four goals start and then nearly catch them up, but with the help of the referee they did just that. With United three goals in the lead at the halfway stage plus one from the first game it looked merely a matter of by how many they would win. But then Red Star rocked them. They swept to the United end like a well-trained army.

Marvellous

Some of their football was marvellous – skill and speed. They used the long ball better than in the first half and it was simply staggering to see United reeling.

What caused this amazing decline? Apart from the referee it was because Red Star had plenty of stamina.

Duncan Edwards kept a pretty close watch on Sekularac in the first half, but it was the home player that did the dictating afterwards and I have seldom seen the England left half play such a minor role.

Foulkes and Byrne stood up manfully to the hammering they got, but United's attack simply faded in the second half. Prior to that Charlton, Taylor and Viollet dovetailed perfectly, Morgans and Scanlon lent them valuable support, but afterwards they too were put right out of their stride.

Roy Cavanagh MBE & Carl Abbott

OLD INTERNATIONAL

Association Football

MANCHESTER UNITED THROUGH ON AGGREGATE

Excitement a-plenty in second half

FROM AN OLD INTERNATIONAL

Figure 77 Manchester Guardian, February 6, 1957

Who would be a weather prophet? At Belgrade today in warm sunshine and on a grass pitch where the last remnants of melting snow produced the effect of an English lawn flecked with daisies, Red Star and Manchester United began a battle of wits and courage and rugged tackling in the second leg of their quarter-final of the European Cup competition. It ended in a draw, 3-3, but as United had already won the first leg at Old Trafford by 2-1 they thus gained the right to pass into the semi-final round of the competition for the second year in succession on a 5-4 aggregate. Much to the relief of the English party, and to the consternation of the 52,000 home spectators, Viollet had the ball in the net past a dumbfounded Beara in 90 seconds. It was a beautifully taken goal – a characteristic effort by that player—but rather lucky in the way that a rebound had run out in United's favour. But as Jones remarked "You need luck at this game": and he could have added, "and a suit of chain mail also would not have come amiss." A second goal almost came fourteen minutes later, delightfully taken by Charlton after a corner kick by Scanlon had been headed on by Viollet, but this was disallowed because of off-side by the Austrian referee, whose performance on the whistle so far had assumed the proportions of a flute obbligato. That was due to the frequency with which fouls were being committed on both sides after Sekularac had set the fashion in shabbiness by stabbing Morgans on the knee. But in spite of the many stops and starts events in the first half ran smoothly for United on whose behalf Taylor led his line like a true hotspur from centre forward. Other factors telling strongly in Manchester's favour at this time were the clean hands and sound judgment of Gregg in goal.

Charlton Scores

Further success for United was impending, Charlton this time was the chosen instrument. Dispossessing Kostic about forty yards from goal, this gifted boy leaned beautifully into his stride, made ground rapidly for about ten yards, then beat one of the finest goalkeepers on the continent with a shot of tremendous power and superb placing. There, one thought, surely goes England's Bloomer of the future. Further evidence of Charlton's claim to that distinction was to emerge two minutes later. A smartly taken free kick got the Red Star defence into a real tangle Edwards fastened on the ball and

72

did his best to oblige his colleagues and supporters, by bursting it (a feat by the way which he was to achieve later): but he muffed his kick this time and the ball rolled to Charlton, apparently lost in a thicket of Red Star defenders. Stalemate surely. But not with Charlton about. His quick eye detected the one sure route through this circle of legs; his trusty boot drove the ball unerringly along it. 3-0 on the day: 5.1 on the aggregate. Nice going. As was natural the Red Star players completely lost their poise.

Their forwards flung themselves heatedly against a defence as firm and steady as a rock; even Sekularac, after a bright beginning in which he showed his undoubted skill, lost heart visibly and stumbled repeatedly. Nevertheless there was an upsurge of the old fighting spirit when Kostic scored a fine goal for Red Star two minutes after half-time. It ought to have been followed by a second one three minutes later when Sekularac placed the ball perfectly for Mitic. Mitic's terrific shot cleared the bar by a foot—no more. Next a curious mix up by Foulkes and Tasic, Red Star's centre forward, ended in Foulkes falling flat on top of Tasic and blotting him completely from view. According to Foulkes, Tasic lost his footing, fell over, and pulled Foulkes over with him, but it looked bad, and the whistle blew at once with attendant gesture indicating a penalty. Tasic had the satisfaction of converting that one, although his shot only just evaded Gregg's finger-tips. The score now was 3-2 and the crowd broke into an uncontrolled frenzy of jubilation and excitement. So much so that when Tasic failed to walk the ball into a goal that was completely unprotected—Gregg was lying hurt and helpless on the ground—a miniature repetition of the Bolton disaster seemed to occur at one corner of the arena. Down the terraces streamed a wild horde of excited spectators eager to help Tasic administer the final touch; and dozens of spectators hung limply along the concrete walls with the breath crushed out of their bodies. If indeed nothing worse had befallen them.

Anxious Moments

A quarter of an hour from the end Red Star, with their confidence and self-respect restored, were wheeling and curvetting, passing and shooting in their best style, and United's defenders had to fight their way out of a regular nightmare of desperate situations. It was significant hereabouts that United's inside forwards were not coming back to chase the ball as they had done so effectively in the first half, and this, of course, threw added pressure on the rear-guard. As soon as this fault was rectified the Red Star attacks, though frequent enough, lost something of their sting. In fact, United began to pile on the pressure at the other end and once Morgans struck a post with a glorious shot. Then we saw as brilliant, and at the same time as unlucky a save as Gregg may ever experience. In dashing out and snatching the ball off the foot of a forward on the fringe of the penalty area, Gregg had the misfortune to roll forward still holding the ball, and so handle it outside the area. Kostic's free kick (according to Viollet) struck the side of Viollet's head and gained thereby such a tricky curve that Gregg could only palm the ball into the net. Three all. Yugoslavians' tails up now with a vengeance, and only one goal required to enforce the dearly sought replay. But only three minutes remained for play, and Jones, Foulkes, Byrne. Edwards, and Colman, who had played magnificently throughout - as had the rest - saw to it that that goal never materialised.

GEORGE FOLLOWS

Two-goal Charlton pips the Slavs

Red Star (Belgrade) 3, Manchester United 3 (United win 5-4 on aggregate)

Figure 78 Daily Herald, February 6, 1958

THE Blue Danube flows grey and cold through this city of Belgrade tonight. And for all Manchester United care referee Karl Kainer of Vienna can jump in it—whistle and all! The Red Devils played the best football they have ever played in serious competition abroad and battled through again to the semi-finals of the European Cup. But they accused Referee Kainer of robbing them of resounding victory before an ultra-partisan crowd at the Partizan Stadium here. HERR KAINER'S STRANGE INTERPRETATIONS OF SOCCER LAWS PITCHED RED STAR DRAMATICALLY BACK INTO THE GAME AFTER THEY HAD BEEN SHAKEN WITH THREE GOALS IN THE FIRST 31 MINUTES. The Slavs surged on this sudden tide of fortune, hit back with two goals in ten minutes of the second half and equalised on the stroke of 90 minutes in a furious finish that ended with United running back to the dressing rooms under a critical chorus of whistles. The referee gave 24 free kicks against United; 11 against Red Star.

Said Manager MATT BUSBY: "He was so bad the lads had to stop playing their normal game." Said Skipper ROGER BYRNE: "We stopped tackling because good tackles were being punished with free kicks."

VIOLLET STRIKES

But the wordy warfare off the field should not obscure a great event of national importance that happened on it. Bobby Charlton, just 20, a member of the great footballing family, proved his true international qualities in the fiery furnace that was the Partizan Stadium. No other English inside-right could have played harder or better or shot straighter or more quickly than did Charlton. He scored twice IN A TEAM WHICH WROTE A GLITTERING TESTIMONY TO OUR FOOTBALL FOR 45 MINUTES, HE AND TOMMY TAYLOR WERE THE STARS.

Within 90 seconds the Slav shout of "Plavi, Plavi" (Up the Blues) were silenced by a Dennis Viollet goal. Taylor charged down a clearance and Viollet carried the ball clear of two desperate tackles before he hit it low past Beara. This was the spur to United to play their best brand of controlled Soccer, even though 19-year-old right-winger Ken Morgans was kicked on the left thigh by Sekularac after five minutes. Morgans, his thigh relieved with whisky at half-time, was always struggling for pace, but still he managed to hit a post with a great left-foot shot and fill his role in the general scheme. But the 30th-minute goal by Charlton was all his own work. He interrupted a foot-juggling act by Kostic, ran the ball three yards forward and hit sensational 25-yard left-footer that even the bounding Beara could not touch. Three minutes more and Charlton scored again. A crisp right foot from 10 yards— after Duncan Edwards had bulldozed through from a free kick. This should have been Charlton's hat-trick. Trigger-quick thinking had earlier put him in the clear to flick Viollet's header into the net. But he had been too quick even for the linesman. Wrongly he was given offside. Still with three goals in the bag at half-time there seemed no need to worry about the goals that had got away. There seemed plenty more to come. There had been so much shooting that eventually Duncan Edwards burst the ball.

EDWARDS 'BOOKED'

Herr Kainer had taken Edwards' name because he begged to differ about a strange decision against Eddie Colman but it didn't seem possible for the referee to save Red Star. How wrong we were. In the 47th minute Colman moved in to tackle Kostic, was palpably obstructed by another player. By the time he had disentangled himself Kostic was shooting into the net. In the 55th minute Tasic fell in the penalty area and Foulkes fell on top of him. The referee gave a penalty and Tasic scored. Now Sekularac, a ball-playing genius of 19 years, began to thread his way past tacklers who had half their minds on the referee. The Red Devils, robbed of their ease and elegance, were curtailed to defence. It was now a desperate game.

With Harry Gregg lying injured and the crowd spilling over the barriers, Tasic flashed the ball into the side netting from six yards. Gregg, bravely whisking the ball away from driving boots, skidded out the area with the ball in his hands. Tasic lobbed the resultant free-kick over the line up and scored off Gregg's hands. Thirty seconds more and then it was time. Time for the Slavs to whistle, time for Matt Busby to go down to the dressing rooms and proudly say: *This was our best performance in the European Cup.'* Give them a cheer against Wolves on Saturday.

TOM JACKSON

IT MAY BE THE SPANIARDS NEXT TIME, BUT . . . *TONIGHT'S SPORT*

United will never have a tougher fight than this!

Figure 79 Manchester Evening News, February 6, 1958

By TOM JACKSON   Belgrade, Thursday.

NOW I'm ready to wager my last Yugoslav dinar that even though it may be the strutting Spaniards of Real Madrid who Manchester United will be set to face in the semi-final of the European Cup, they will never have a tougher fight on their hands than the one they survived here against the challenge of Red Star.

Believe me, this match that ended with the rivals gaining three goals each and United through to the last-four stage by the barest possible goal margin on aggregate had everything to send the blood running fast through the veins.

How else but by sheer, at times almost desperate, determination and drive, the deafening roars of 50.000 people ringing in their ears—and some remarkably strange decisions by the Austrian referee -- could Red Star have pulled back three goals and got within sight of forcing a replay. It wasn't that the United defence cracked. It wasn't because the forwards, brilliant in the first half, faded out of the game, to my mind the pendulum swung in Red Star's favour directly they took full toll from a penalty kick which I am sure nine out of 10 referees wouldn't have given.

Ironic

How ironic that big Bill Foulkes, who had an outstanding game at right back, should have conceded the penalty when he made what seemed to me a perfectly legitimate tackle on Red Star Centre-Forward Tasic. From that moment onwards the Yugoslavs were able to come back into the game with a chance of saving the match because the United players seemed dubious about going hard into the tackle in case they might be penalised further.

Even Harry Gregg, who stole much of the thunder of the mighty Beara, swears he chested and did not handle the ball in the incident which led to Red Star scoring their goal in the danger minutes.

But the real story of this full blooded European cup ties is not so much how United had their backs to the wall in the second half, but how they virtually made sure of victory by an inspired forward display in the opening half.

No Panic

Here was the United in their greatest and most polished mood of the season. With Tommy Taylor the architect-in-chief, and young Bobby Charlton—the best forward on the field— and Dennis Viollet the goal snatching spearheads. Taylor didn't hit the goal trail, but he worked and polished tremendously hard in keeping the line moving.

And the defence: Well three goals against might suggest they panicked under the weight of Red Star's heavy pressure. Not a bit of it. Gregg, Foulkes, Mark Jones, and Roger Byrne never lost their beads in matching the Yugoslav forwards, who put much more bite into their play than they did in the first leg at Old Trafford.

Foulkes takes top marks because he was the coolest and surest United defender all through the game, Eddie Colman had a splendid first half, but he was out of touch when the battle waged thickest later on, and Duncan Edwards was much below the rip-roaring form he showed at Old Trafford in curbing the activities of inside-forward Sekularac. The Yugoslav "wonder boy" had a much brighter game before his own fans: but some of the shine was lost because his tackling was often too robust.

It was only the spirit and courage of young Morgans that kept him going after taking a nasty knock above the knee in the first few minutes— an injury which puts him in doubt for Saturday's top of the table League tussle with the Wolves. The only other United casualty was Duncan Edwards, who has an ankle injury, but he is expected to be fit for Saturdays game. That's the story at Belgrade —a battle that will be long remembered in this European Cup which has produced so many tense and dramatic struggles for United.

ARCHIE LEDBROOKE

BABES SNOWBALLED BY RED STAR FANS

From ARCHIE
LEDBROOKE
Belgrade, Wednesday.

Figure 80 Daily Mirror, February 6, 1958

RED STAR **3**
Rostic (47 and 89 mins.), Tasic (pen.—55 mins.).

MANCHESTER UNITED . . . **3**
Viollet (2 mins.), Charlton (30 and 32 mins.).
United won 5—4 on aggregate.

The Busby Babes are angry young men tonight. Their delight at reaching the European Cup semi-finals for the second, successive year, is tempered by the hostile treatment they had from the 52,000 Belgrade fans. They were given the bird with the shrill whistle which is the Continental equivalent of the English boo. And at the end they walked off in a shower of snowballs.

The fans' enthusiasm was fanned into flames- by Austrian referee Karl Kainer. He repeatedly gave free-kicks against tackles which are considered fair in England. Kainer gave thirty-five free kicks for fouls — twenty-four of them against United. Duncan Edwards had his name taken when he shouted in protest after Eddie Colman had been obstructed and had a free kick given against him. Skipper Roger Byrne said later: "We just stopped tackling. We dare not go in."

Hard Pressed

So brilliant United, after leading 3—0 at half time through Viollet (2m.) and Charlton (30m. and 32m.), were hard pressed to save the tie. The rough stuff was started by Sekularac, the Yugoslav wonder boy, who was suspended for five months last season. He kicked Ken Morgans on the leg in the first few minutes. When Morgans went in at half-time his leg was so painful he could not sit. Whisky was poured over it to numb the pain and he bravely came out for the second half. Red Star struck. Quickly; Kostlc scored with a long cross shot. In the fifty-fifth minute Tasic scored from a penalty after being tackled by Bill Foulkes. Then, in the very last minute, goalkeeper Harry Gregg fell outside his area and handled the ball. The free kick was a slow chip shot, but it hit Viollet and spun away from Gregg into the net.

HENRY ROSE

From HENRY ROSE
Belgrade, Wednesday
Red Star 3 Man. Utd. 3
Manchester go to semi-finals on 5—4 winning aggregate.

Busby boys beat fans, referee, and Red Star

Figure 81 Daily Express, February 6, 1958

Manchester United added another shining page to their glittering history here in Belgrade today. They reached the semi-final of the European Cup for a second season despite inflamed Yugoslavs, one-sided refereeing and injuries. The injuries - to Duncan Edwards and Ken Morgans - forced United, who led 3-0 at half-time, to lead a magnificent rear-guard action. Some decisions by Austrian referee Karl Keiner were Double Dutch to me.

Out of Focus. The second half was tough but the tally of 24 free kicks against United and 11 against Red Star was completely out of focus. The climax to Herr Kainer's interpretations, which helped inflame the crowd against United, came in the 55th minute when he gave a penalty against Billy Foulkes. Nothing is wrong with my eyesight - and Foulkes confirmed what I saw – a Red Star player had slipped and pulled United's star defender down with him. A joke of a ruling it would have been if Tasic had not scored from the spot. I found it easy in this white hot battle to forgive Duncan Edwards protesting over a free kick. The referee took Edwards number.

At the start of the game, only 90 seconds had gone when centre-half Spajic fluffed a clearance. The ball hit Tommy Taylor, rebounded to Dennis Viollet who scored. The excited crowd were starting violent vocal action, but Charlton silenced them with two goals in three minutes. First a left-foot drive in the 28th minute, then a right-footer as right-back Tomic all but boobed his clearance. You can't do that sort of thing with Charlton around and so it was 3-0-5-1 on aggregate and an hour to go. All over. It seemed.

"We were 3 up at Highbury on Saturday" said someone. Before we had laughed that one off Tasic had scored for Red Star with a 20 yard drive in the 47th minute. Then came that fantastic penalty – 3-2 now and backs to the wall while Red Star inside-forwards Sekularac and Kostic, a pair worth £100,000 performed wonders. Harry Gregg was hurt, Morgans and Edwards limping, Roger Byrne was warned for wasting time and United players were penalised for harmless looking tackles.

Last Seconds. I thought Herr Kainer would have given a free kick when one of the ball boys fell over. There were only seconds to go when United lined up for a free kick, awarded against Gregg for handling the ball outside the penalty area. Kostic's shot hit Viollet's head and the leaping Gregg could only palm the ball into the net. A fantastic recovery by Red Star—3-3 and only 5-4 on aggregate.

ERIC THOMPSON

No-tackle ref scares United

By ERIC THOMPSON
BELGRADE, Wednesday.
Red Star ...3 Manchester U. 1

Figure 82 Daily Mail, February 6, 1958

AFTER all the adventures involved in reaching the European Cup semi-final for the second year in succession, Manchester United don't scare easily. But they were nearly scared into a replay today by Austrian referee Karl Kainer – pronounced mud in Manchester touring circles.

Two Red Star goals came from bad decisions and United players in the dressing room admitted in this nerve wracking return tie (they won the first 2 —I) that they became frightened of making a tackle.

This was especially so after the 55th minute, when a penalty was awarded against Foulkes for an alleged foul on Red Star centre-forward Tasic.

Phobia

In my opinion, the decision was wrong. Tasic scored from the spot, to reduce the United's half-time lead of 3-0 to 3-2. I say emphatically, that this was not a dirty game. Yet the whistling Austrian with the anti-tackling phobia awarded 24 free kicks against United with 11 against Red Star. I thought his eyesight amiss too in the incident that led the Red Star goal in the last minute. Centre-forward Tasic had limped off. Kostic was foiled by Gregg's despairing dive at his feet. Gregg slid outside of the penalty area, the ball under him, and he made sure not to use his hands, when he rose to kick clear. But, a free-kick for handling was given. Kostic chipped and the ball touched Viollet's head before going into the net.

Unhappy Edwards

Kostic tall and dangerously accurate had scored Red Star's first goal, two minutes after a first-half Edwards will remember all his life. He ricked an ankle. Had the referee's notebook flashed in his face for talking, burst the ball with a shot that was blocked, yet travelled 25 yards, made a sloppy shot that led to Charlton goal.

I made little Colman the most consistent of the winning team. Edwards never hit his Old Trafford form. Viollet was struggling, though he took the opening goal, after two minutes, superbly. Charlton pounded a 22 yard shot past Beara after 29 minutes. His second after 32 minutes, followed a free-kick.

THE YUGOSLAV VIEW

Before leaving the match reports and considering the events that followed, an interesting counterpoint to the British match reports is provided by the Manchester Evening News which consistently included reports and views from journalists form the country in which United played. The (unnamed) Yugoslav journalist that reported for 'Politika' had a very different view of the match:

'United were unsportsmanlike and often unscrupulous. In the second-half the British players felled opponents in an impermissible manner. Many times we asked ourselves where the renowned British fair play was. That is only a legend. There was not a single professional trick that they did not use to bring themselves out of difficult positions, and were often unscrupulous when they tackled, and pushed and tripped.'

While no doubt the comment is laced with a degree of home bias, it is perhaps an indication that the Babes were gaining the experience, guile and know how to go all the way in the competition.

'THE LAST JOURNEY'

Thursday, February 6 was certainly milder than when the party had arrived on the Monday and there was one or two tender heads after the celebrations of the previous night as they returned to the Zenum airport in Belgrade for the first leg of the return journey to Manchester via Munich. A relatively quiet journey saw them land in bitterly cold weather with thick snow lying around the place. Making their way to the Munich airport buildings, through the sleet lashing the face and walking through the snow for some refreshments and time for journalists to send their copy back to Manchester, the break of about an hour saw everyone in great heart as they knew they were heading back home.

The plane set off down the runway before the two pilots spotted an uneven engine sound so returned back down the runway. A second attempt to take off saw the same thing happen forty seconds on the way with the plane coming to a halt down the runway. Captain Rayment assured everybody this was just a technical hitch and that they would need to disembark and return to the airport buildings. It seemed to a lot of people that this might be a long delay, even an overnight stay in Munich would be needed.

In a surprising short time, the call was given to return to the plane and set off back to Manchester. The party resumed sitting where they wanted to sit, no official seating places with those wanting a quiet time seemingly going to the front, whilst all the press corps, except Frank Taylor, went to the tail end with a card school being on their agenda. Frank intended joining them once airborne for the flight back home. I say all the press corps but one was missing as the head count of passengers was made, Alf Clarke. At that moment though, a red faced Alf was running as fast as he could across to reach the plane, panting away obviously upset as well that he had caused a delay. Alf Clarke, therefore, was the last person to speak to anybody in England before the crash. Once on board all the players and his journalist friends quickly were shouting at him, but in a good natured way, as he was a well-respected man who had Manchester United red blood running through him. Alf had actually been sending the last message back to Manchester to warn of the delay and, even, a possible overnight stay in Munich, and also getting a message to his wife that he would still hope to be attending the annual Press Ball that had been arranged in Manchester for that Thursday night.

This time the plane rolled further along the runway, the time was 15-04pm, the surge that had happened in the previous two attempts returned but frantically the pilots noticed the air speed indicator dropping from 117 knots down to 105 and both realised, that this time there was no stopping, they were too far down the runway and knew they would not rise through the obstacles that lay ahead. Those who survived recall the horrendous noise, where everything seemed to turn upside down with an awful sound of tearing, ripping, smoke and flames.

The Manchester United team, Britain's elite journalists had crashed at the end of Munich airport runway with catastrophic result. How the news was heard by the press back in Manchester is recounted by John Roberts in his excellent book The Team That Wouldn't Die:

'By six o'clock in the busy press rooms all around Manchester, the news was still not being taken in, but the news had to get out to the many who relied so much on newspapers for all information in those times. The news kept being shouted out, first in one office then the various offices ringing each other, 'No, not young Eddie Colman' 'surely not Tommy Taylor' and then Roger Byrne, Mark Jones, Geoff Bent, David Pegg, Finally, 'No not that shy lad Billy Whelan, how could this happen to him, he never harmed anybody not even an opponent'. When the devastating news came through about their fellow journalists it was a time for grown men to cry unashamedly. 'Poor Alf Clarke, he watched United so often that when a red was kicked Alf limped' 'And dear old Tom Jackson, never harmed anybody in his life' 'neither did Eric Thompson, he would help anybody' 'No, not George Follows, how could a talent like that be wiped out?' 'Archie Ledbrooke, always burning his hand on my cigarettes, you should start smoking Archie I had said, smokers never burn their hands on other peoples cigarettes!' 'Why have we not heard about Henry Rose or Donny Davies?' 'We have, both are on fatalities list' 'No not Henry, it can't be' 'Donny? And poor old Swifty's gone'

Alf Clarke, Henry Rose and Donny Davies had lived through the fire and fury of two world wars, George Follows, Tom Jackson, Eric Thompson, Archie Ledbrooke and Frank Swift all battle hardened by the second world war, Davies had also been a Prisoner of War in Germany and Jackson working behind enemy lines in Germany, and there today, at the end of a German runway would be their last call in life.

The City of Manchester was a hushed place of genuine sadness, only the main arteries seeming to function. The Cathedral held a service, whist the Halle, conducted by Barbiroli, played 'Nimrod' the musicians traditional tribute to dead colleagues.

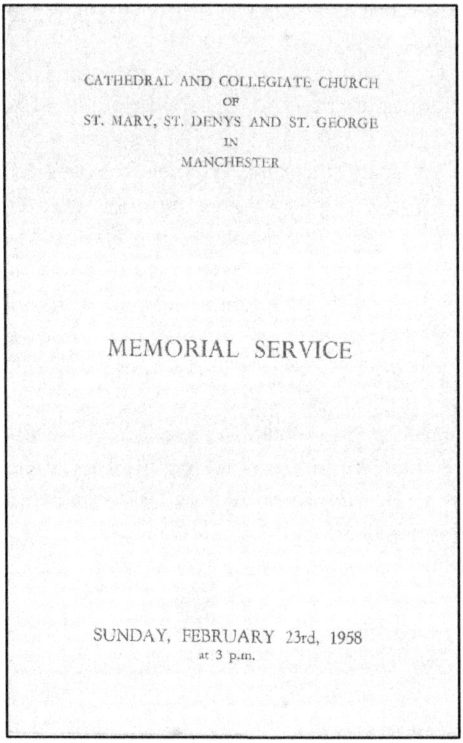

CATHEDRAL AND COLLEGIATE CHURCH
OF
ST. MARY, ST. DENYS AND ST. GEORGE
IN
MANCHESTER

MEMORIAL SERVICE

SUNDAY, FEBRUARY 23rd, 1958
at 3 p.m.

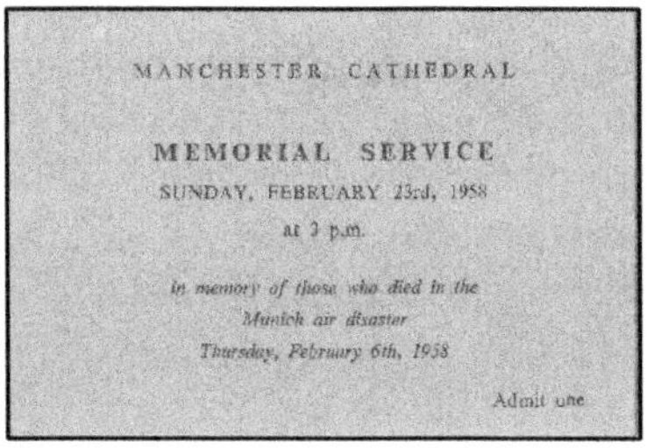

MANCHESTER CATHEDRAL

MEMORIAL SERVICE
SUNDAY, FEBRUARY 23rd, 1958
at 3 p.m.

In memory of those who died in the
Munich air disaster
Thursday, February 6th, 1958

Admit one

Figure 83 Memorial Service, Manchester Cathedral

CHAPTER SEVEN
THE PRESS CORP THAT SURVIVED

FRANK TAYLOR JOURNALIST - 'NEWS CHRONICLE'

Over the years Roy Cavanagh has had the real honour and pleasure to speak to virtually all the Cricket Societies in Britain, from the Scotland Society which has meetings in Glasgow and Edinburgh, all the way down to the South Coast at Hove in Sussex. They all follow the same pattern, an audience of avid cricket lovers interested to hear what the speaker can bring to their attention that they did not know, which not much is! You are expected to speak for about forty minutes then a break, then about half hour question and answer. Finally, a member of the audience gives, hopefully, a vote of thanks. Roy recalls the following story with a mixture of pride and astonishment

'One of my visits to Yorkshire took me in the early 1990's to a place a lot of people would pronounce as WOMBWELL but Yorkshire folk are quite insistent it is WOMWELL. It was to the town's working man type club close to Barnsley that I went to give my usual talk. Although it is expected to be cricket orientated, I do mention my football books with stories about Matt Busby, Duncan Edwards, and George Best etc as they are well known to all. On this particular night, the vote of thanks was given by a small, moustached man, who quite simply said I knew all those people, he then introduced himself, it was FRANK TAYLOR, the only journalist to survive the Munich air crash. I was genuinely shocked and could not remember what he said as I was in the midst of somebody I seemed to know all about yet had not met. It was truly an honour for me.'

Born in Barrow, it was at the local grammar school that John Frederick Taylor, soon to be known as Frank, would have a love of writing, joining the local Barrow Guardian when he left education. Spending the Second World War in the Royal Air Force stopped that, but on being demobbed it was a move across to a Sheffield newspaper before he joined the News Chronicle in 1953.

Married to Peggy, they had two sons Andrew and Alastair. It was Andrew's full name of, Andrew MacDonald Taylor, which caused real confusion as to whether or not Frank Taylor had been killed or survived the Munich air crash. In all the consternation and debris, a page of a passport showed the name 'Andrew MacDonald' with the surname burned off. It was that scrap of paper which gave hope to the family as they realised it would be too much of a coincidence for there to be an actual Andrew MacDonald aboard the fated aeroplane. Frank Taylor was alive, the only journalist of the nine who boarded the plane in Munich to be so.

As the team boarded the plane for the third time, Frank turned to outside left Albert Scanlon and said, "In the RAF, if you didn't take off at the first attempt, the flight was cancelled!" I just sensed the danger coming fast and told anybody near me to 'get your head between your knees' then everything went black. I came around with a massive wheel seemingly covering me, looked and saw my best suit covered in blood and dirt and just thought 'my wife is not going to be happy with me'. I passed out and, unbeknown to me of course, my name was put on the missing list, presumed dead. Meanwhile I was in a German Catholic Hospital where they kept me for several weeks, at one time with even the possibility of having a leg amputated. My doctor was a marvellous man, I said to him as I was leaving the hospital, 'What a crazy world, only a few years ago we were trying to kill each other and now you save my life.' The doctor said to me,' Frank what you don't realise is when you were unconscious I gave you a transfusion of German fraulein blood!'

Two other men with a journalistic theme who survived the crash were both Daily Mail employees.

TED ELLYARD; TELEGRAPHIST

Being a Telegraphist was one of the first 'high technology' professions in the modern era. It enables the operator to send and receive the Morse code in order to communicate by landlines or radio. So, you can imagine how vital such a person would be in the 1950's as the reports were urgently needed to be sent back home.

Ted was immediately recognised by his handle bar moustache, which confirmed your instant thought that he was an ex R.A.F. man. Along with his colleague, Peter Howard, Ted was a hero of Munich, going back into the plane to help the survivors.

PETER HOWARD; PHOTOGRAPHER

Peter Howard was closer to the partisan Belgrade crowd than anyone as he attempted to record the action via his camera, which with six goals flying in had quite a bit! At one stage the crowd's enthusiasm at the comeback of the Red Star team from 0-3 down to 3-3 caused a crowd surge with many crashing through the netting separating them from the pitch.

I SAW GOALIE GREGG LEAD THE RESCUERS

By PETER HOWARD

Daily Mail cameraman, reporting from the crash scene at Munich within an hour of crawling from the wreckage.

Figure 84 Daily Mail, February 7, 1958

There would be many heroes of Munich, it is only right that the name of Peter Howard is mentioned at the top of the list as, in the words of Captain Thain later when his name was mentioned said, *'God...that chap had guts'*. Writing in the Daily Mail on the day after the crash, this is how Peter recalled the crash:

Peter Howard, barefoot, phones his story from the airport. He is 30, married, with three children, has travelled thousands of miles covering United's games.

Figure 85 Daily Mail, February 7, 1958

'I can't remember if there was a bang or not. Everything stopped all at once. I was so dazed that I just scrambled about. Then I found that Ted Elyard and I were still together. We found a hole in the wreckage. We crawled out on our hands and knees. As soon as I got clear my first instinct was, quite frankly, to run away. I was terrified. But I managed somehow to stay put. I turned round and there was Harry Gregg the goalkeeper, who also managed to get out. He seemed to be unhurt too. Anyway his voice was in working order for he was shouting: "Come on lads. Let's get stuck in."

That got us going. Gregg, Ted Elyard, the two stewardesses, the radio operator and myself went back into the wreckage. It was a terrible mess. It made me want to shut my eyes. I saw Captain Thain getting hold of a small fire extinguisher. He started putting out small fires. I started looking if there was anyone I knew. I saw Captain Rayment trapped in the cockpit, but he was got out. A Yugoslav woman passenger and her small baby were pulled clear by the radio operator, Mr Rodgers. I remember getting Frank Taylor, sports writer of the News Chronicle out. He was badly hurt. We also got Ray Wood out and one or two others. Bodies were strewn in the snow for 150 yards. I went to look for Eric Thompson. I could see no sign of him. I am just realising what an awful thing it is......

CHAPTER EIGHT
THE JOURNALISTS THAT FOLLOWED

On the emotional night of Wednesday February 19, 1958, a mere two weeks since Manchester United had battled through an hostile environment in Belgrade to qualify for the semi-final of the European Cup for the second successive season, a packed out Old Trafford, with thousands locked outside, had gathered to see how the 'new' Manchester United would cope in the FA Cup 5th round tie against Sheffield Wednesday.

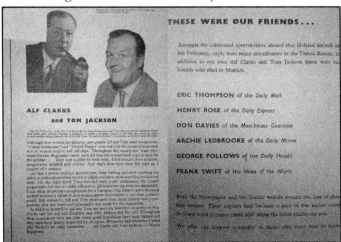

Figure 86 Journalists remembered, United Review, February 19, 1958

Seven players had already been killed, forty-eight hours after this tie another, felt by many to be even then at the young age of twenty one, one of the world's great players, Duncan Edwards, would die from his injuries. Only two of the side that had played two weeks previously, Harry Gregg and Billy Foulkes were able to play, the other nine who took the field included players such as Ian Greaves, Freddie Goodwin, Ronnie Cope, Colin Webster and Alex Dawson who had appeared at first team level before, along with two rushed signings, the experienced former Newcastle United, Blackpool and England player Ernie Taylor and a left half signed from Aston Villa Stan Crowther, who actually had played in the previous FA Cup Final against United and had also already appeared in the competition this season for Villa, thus becoming the only person to play for two sides in the same season in the FA Cup. The other two players, making their debut were youngsters, inside forward Mark Pearson and outside left Shay Brennan.

That Manchester United had encountered massive problems in even putting out a side, the newspaper industry was also in chaos as they had to replace nine journalists of complete knowledge of the club, the game, and the players. David Meek for the Manchester Evening News and Keith Dewhurst for the Manchester Evening Chronicle, also had the unenviable task of being in the front line nightly as their papers tried to convey the feeling in the club, the surge of emotion around Manchester and what was happening still back in Munich, where only one of the nine journalists who had made the trip, Frank Taylor, was alive and he was fighting for his life after his extensive injuries.

David Meek had been in the Manchester Evening News offices on the Thursday as news came through about the crash that afternoon. He remembered the banging of the hatch through which reports from Reuters and the Press Association sent their dispatches, particularly remembering the very loud banging as very important news was coming through which would be out of the ordinary. David would not realise that he was soon to be elevated as the man to do the day to day reporting for a Manchester United, who could never be the same club as they were before the crash.

As David, and the other reporters, some who may have had only occasional reporting of sporting events, gathered in the Old Trafford press box on the night of the Sheffield Wednesday cup tie, they had the usual task of around 500 words plus the team lists. He would witness emotion that he possibly would not encounter again in what would, eventually, turn out to be an incredible thirty nine years of covering Manchester United. Two goals from the debut lad Shay Brennan, one direct from a corner, and another from Alex Dawson would give United an incredible 3-0 victory and continue their FA Cup adventures.

David Meek recalled his first meeting with Matt Busby after he returned to Old Trafford later in the season. *I was introduced to Matt at a hotel before a United game. He looked very sad, and seeing such as Peter Slingsby (who quite quickly had replaced Keith Dewhurst at the Chronicle) and myself, seemed to make him sadder as he remembered there would be no more Alf Clarke and Tom Jackson. It also reminded myself of the task that faced me. A while later, Peter and I were in Europe with the team. It was a real feeling of the creating of a bond between us, something vital in relationships between manager and press. Matt came up to us both and said, "I don't know how much travelling abroad you have done, but in case you haven't had the chance, here is some local currency for you."* Time was moving on…

It is incredible to think that, sixty years since the crash, only David Meek for 39 years and then Stuart Matheson for 21 years have covered Manchester United for the Manchester Evening News. David Meek also wrote numerous books on the club, all with an in depth authority. He could never have envisaged that Thursday afternoon that he would be in the Old Trafford press box for the first time on February 22. He went on to follow the club brilliantly over those next thirty nine years.

The National newspapers, of course, had to also promote or realign reporters to cover the ongoing football scene. There were, however, stories of those who might have been on the fated flight. Frank McGhee, as mentioned, nearly had gone instead of Archie Ledbrooke, John Arlott instead of Donny Davies and Geoffrey Green who wrote for The Times had also expected to be on the flight but his paper detailed him to cover the important World Cup tie in Cardiff between Wales and Israel. An interesting point, Geoffrey Green gave the eulogy at the end of February 1958 to his departed colleagues at St. Bride's Church in Fleet Street, London before a packed congregation. The then England manager, and former Manchester United player, Walter Winterbottom, read the second address.

Those three, McGhee, Arlott and Green would become noted journalists, and in Arlott's case, a marvellous broadcaster, particularly on cricket. Others who would become worthy followers of the men cruelly lost at Munich would be such as Arthur Walmsley, Steve Richards, Desmond Hackett and John Roberts, whilst Peter Slingsby would quite quickly take on the Manchester Evening Chronicle role off Keith Dewhurst, before the Chronicle would cease publication in the summer of 1962.

CLOSING THOUGHTS.

Two teams died at the end of Munich airports runway on 6th February 1958. One a Manchester United football team who already had excelled and had the real potential to have become one of the game's greatest ever sides. Commonly known as the 'Busby Babes' or the 'Red Devils', they were still a young, vibrant team dominating in England and into their second season on foreign fields. Their draw in Belgrade on February 5, 1958 had put them into their second European Cup Semi-Final. They were close to the league leaders Wolverhampton Wanderers at the top of the old First Division, chasing a treble of league titles, whilst a 5th round FA Cup tie against Sheffield Wednesday at home beckoned.

The crash at the end of the Munich airport runway stopped that side from achieving its goal; it nearly stopped Manchester United itself, as a lack of players and financial burdens threatened the whole fabric of the club. On the Saturday before the crash, United had played an incredible match at Highbury against Arsenal, whilst two hundred miles away in Manchester their reserve side had played a game against Wolverhampton Wanderers. Of the twenty-two United players in action that day, only eight would really be fit to play football for the rest of the season. Eight truly incredible players lost their lives, whilst a further two would never play again.

How do you handle all that?

In our opinion, but for one man, Jimmy Murphy, Manchester United might very well not have carried on. Ten years later they would win the European Cup! Thirty One years on an incredible treble of League, FA. Cup AND European Cup was achieved. Today they hold the record of Twenty league titles, numerous FA Cup Final victories, a few League Cups (or whatever it is called these days!) more European trophies and World Club Championships. They are as famous as any football side in the world.

On the same flight home from Belgrade via Munich, were the cream of football journalists. Nine men whose columns were read eagerly every day of the week, their words taken as gospel for what was going on in sport. Indeed, the whole context of this book is a time when journalists were as, if not more, famous than the footballers they reported on. Sadly, despite what we are sure are the best efforts of today's journalists, reporting is often no longer about what happens on the football pitch, but off it, as any element of a story, true or otherwise, likely to sell papers is sought. Back in 1958 what went on away from the pitch stayed amongst those that were there. Now, social media has arrived and stories true or otherwise, are out there before journalists have time to, metaphorically, put pen to paper as the stories continue to grow by the minute. In response, newspapers, once the sole source of information for the masses are now also online as they battle to save their art against the continuing rise of this unmediated social media.

Eight of the finest journalists died alongside the players they knew better than anybody. A ninth, Frank Taylor, survived and went onto have a great career. Seven footballers would survive, one of them Bobby Charlton, would achieve everything there is to achieve in the game. Other truly great footballers would arrive, and many truly great journalists would ply their profession. Whether the world in which they lived was a better or worse place is of course a matter of opinion. Whether the journalists or footballers that followed would have matched those on the plane that day is another question that cannot be answered. What is beyond dispute though, is that the disaster at Munich robbed the world of true greatness, both on the pitch and off it. We hope that in reading this book you will share our admiration, not only for the great players whose careers were so cruelly cut short, but also, for the journalists that so brilliantly immortalised those Busby Babes in print.

List of Figures

Picture Credits are as follows:

Figures from Daily Mirror, Manchester Evening News, Manchester Evening Chronicle and Daily Herald with permission of Trinity Mirror. Figures from Manchester Guardian with permission of The Guardian. Figures from Daily Express with permission of Express Newspapers Figures from the News of the World with permission of News Licensing

Team photo (front cover) scanpix.

Figures 1,19, 20, 23, 54, 69 74 & 83 from the Leslie Millman collection, www.flickr.com/photos/manchesterunitedman1/sets

Figure 14 David Jack

ABOUT THE AUTHORS

ROY CAVANAGH MBE

Born in Salford, Roy first saw Manchester United play in 1954. He has contributed to the club programme for six seasons during the 1980's and has had various books on the club and its players published, to date, 20 books including some on Lancashire County Cricket Club. Roy is also an accomplished after dinner speaker and compere. He is married to Barbara, they have two sons, Duncan and Martin- three grandchildren, Claire, Sam and Evie and three great grandchildren, Aila, Harvey and Phoebe.

CARL ABBOTT

Carl Abbott is Professor of Construction Innovation at the University of Salford. Carl is lucky enough to have been born into a family that is Manchester United through and through. His grandfather, Lawrence, was a steward and season ticket holder as were his father, Roy, and aunt, Ann. So too are his three brothers Roy, Mark and John. His first games were as a young boy in the early 70s, and he has had the honour of following United home and away both domestically and in Europe since that time.

Printed in Great Britain
by Amazon

42576706R00059